HIGHER
Business Management

Craig McLeod

HODDER
GIBSON
AN HACHETTE UK COMPANY

Dedication

I would like to thank the following people for their helping me, either directly or indirectly, in writing this book:

Hugh Donnelly, Director at Co-operative Education Trust Scotland for his input into the democratic enterprises topic.

Kieron Gallagher, Head of Business Development for Science & Strategy at SEPA for his assistance and guidance with the SEPA case study and other topics in this book.

Rhona Sivewright, Principal Assessor of Higher Business Management and the rest of the Higher team, for their years of guidance and support through my various roles in the SQA.

Business Education staff at both Lochgelly and Auchmuty High Schools for their support, friendship and teaching me everything I know!

Claire Spinks at Hodder Gibson and Kirsty Taylor for making everything run so smoothly.

Last, but by no means least, my wife Debbie for endless hours of proofreading and moral support!

The Publishers would like to thank the following for permission to reproduce copyright material:

Photo credits

p. 7 Jamie Oliver's Fifteen, Photo © David Loftus; **p. 8** © The Co-operative Group; **p. 11** © Lush Digital; **p. 16** © Procter & Gamble; **p. 33** © Findlay/Alamy; **p. 46** © AVAVA – Fotolia.com; **p. 63** © Rawpixel – Fotolia.com; **p. 65** *top* © Unison; *bottom* © Unite the Union; **p. 96** © Courtesy of Nestle S.A. of Vevey, Switzerland; **p. 104** *top* © Tesco PLC; *bottom* © Reproduced by kind permission of Sainsbury's Supermarkets Ltd; **p. 119** © Justin Kaseztwoz / Alamy; **p. 122** © Everett Collection Historical / Alamy; **p. 123** © Small Town Studio – Fotolia.com; **p. 127** © BSI Group **p. 129** © Cruelty Free International; **p. 130** © Velvet, SCA Group.

Acknowledgements

SQA Outcomes and Assessment Standards adapted by the author and used with permission – copyright © Scottish Qualifications Authority.

Every effort has been made to trace all copyright holders, but if any have been inadvertently overlooked the Publishers will be pleased to make the necessary arrangements at the first opportunity.

Although every effort has been made to ensure that website addresses are correct at time of going to press, Hodder Gibson cannot be held responsible for the content of any website mentioned in this book. It is sometimes possible to find a relocated web page by typing in the address of the home page for a website in the URL window of your browser.

Hachette Livre UK's policy is to use papers that are natural, renewable and recyclable products and made from wood grown in sustainable forests. The logging and manufacturing processes are expected to conform to the environmental regulations of the country of origin.

Orders: please contact Bookpoint Ltd, 130 Park Drive, Milton Park, Abingdon, Oxon OX14 4SE.

Telephone: (44) 01235 827720. Fax: (44) 01235 400454 Lines are open 9.00–5.00, Monday to Saturday, with a 24-hour message answering service. Visit our website at www.hoddereducation.co.uk. Hodder Gibson can be contacted direct on: Tel: 0141 333 4650; Fax: 0141 404 8188; email: hoddergibson@hodder.co.uk

© Craig McLeod 2015

First published in 2015 by
Hodder Gibson, an imprint of Hodder Education,
An Hachette UK Company,
211 St Vincent Street
Glasgow G2 5QY

Impression number   5 4

Year   2019 2018 2017 2016

Cover photo © dashadima – Fotolia
Illustrations by Barking Dog Art Design and Illustration
Typeset in Cronos Pro Light 13/15pt by Aptara, Inc.
Printed in India
A catalogue record for this title is available from the British Library
ISBN: 978 1 4718 3600 8

Contents

The book you are holding is from a second (or subsequent) printing of this title, which has been updated following amendments to the SQA marking scheme for this subject. Additionally, in line with the SQA's expansion of certain areas of the course, further text on 'technology grouping', 'assessing the effectiveness of a decision' and forms of 'on-the-job training' has been added, along with changes to certain key terms.

Introduction

Welcome to *How to Pass Higher Business Management*. This book has been written specifically to prepare you for the new Higher Business Management course. It will help you pass the unit assessments, coursework assignment and question paper set by the Scottish Qualifications Authority (SQA). However, that doesn't mean you have to *learn* everything in this book or indeed that this book contains *everything* you could possibly need to know in an assessment situation. If you haven't realised already, Higher Business Management is a dynamic (this means always changing) course that is relevant to real life. In other words, there are endless possibilities when it comes to answering questions that can be exemplified by your own experiences of business as well as what you study in this book.

The subject

What do you mean, you have no experience of business? Of course you do! Every time you go into a shop, watch a TV advert or surf the internet for new clothes, you are engaging with *business*. Perhaps you have a part-time job or have taken part in work experience at school? These experiences will stand you in good stead when studying Higher Business Management.

Higher Business Management has grown in popularity over recent years. Many students like it for the reasons outlined above, that is, it is relevant to real life and interesting enough to pass the time with at school. Another reason why it is so popular, especially with those students 'crashing' the subject (that is attempting the Higher without having studied National 5), is because the course assumes no previous knowledge. There are some subjects that you have been studying since you were five. Sometimes it is difficult to attempt a Higher in something you have found tough throughout your school life. Well, the great thing about Business Management is that because the subject material is constantly being updated and is taught from scratch by your teacher each year, everyone starts at the same point, engaging with content that is relevant to them. As long as you are hard-working, revisit the day's lesson at home each night and listen to your teacher's advice, you will pass the course! Oh, and make sure you endeavour to write in proper sentences, too!

How to use this book

The book contains a number of features that are designed to help you make the most of your studies. They are:

The course

The Higher Business Management course is split into three units:
- Unit 1: Understanding Business
- Unit 2: Management of People and Finance
- Unit 3: Management of Marketing and Operations

This book has seven main chapters which cover the knowledge and understanding, and the mandatory skills required for each unit.

Course assessment

The course assessment for Higher Business Management is made up of two components:

1 Question paper (70 marks, 70% of overall grade).
2 Coursework assignment (30 marks, 30% of overall grade).

Question paper

The **question paper** is set by the SQA and will be taken during the main examination diet. The exam is *closed book*, so you won't have access to notes or books.

The question paper is designed to give you the opportunity to apply your knowledge and understanding of business concepts from all topics in the course. This is your chance to show the examiner what you are made of! You should be ready for this, even excited to get in there and have the chance to pull together a year of studying to get the grade you deserve!

The question paper has two sections:

Section 1 (30 marks): This is known as a 'case study' and will be made up of a main case study text with *exhibits* containing additional information. This section will consist of *mandatory* short answer questions (that is you must answer *all* of them), each worth between 1 and 6 marks, based on the case study.

Remember

Questions will require you to *demonstrate* your skills, knowledge and understanding from studying the course AND your ability to *apply* them to the case study. In other words, all the answers are not contained in the case study and exhibits provided – you will need to draw on relevant material from your studies. Likewise, you will not get full marks if you just regurgitate knowledge from your studies without applying it to the context of the case study and questions.

Section 2 (40 marks): This section will consist of four, 10-mark questions based on one of the following areas: Understanding Business, Management of People, Management of Finance, Management of Marketing or Management of Operations.

Command words

Command words are used in each question in the question paper (and the unit assessments too). The command word is the first word of the question and is designed to guide you to answer the question in the way in which it is intended to be answered.

Below is a list of the *common* command words used in Higher Business Management questions with advice on how you should tackle them. Further hints and tips on how to interpret command words can be found in the Answers to exam-style questions section at the end of this book.

Command word	Explanation	Hints and tips
Identify (Only used in unit assessments)	Present in brief form.	Simply name or state. No detailed description is required.
Outline (Only used in unit assessments)	Provide a brief summary of content.	More than identifying, but not a detailed description.
Describe	Make a number of relevant factual points, e.g. characteristics and/or features.	Write descriptions in full sentences. These are more than just 'outlines' of facts.
Discuss	Communicate issues, ideas or information that make a case for and/or against.	Describe advantages/disadvantages, costs/benefits, etc. Use the link word 'however' to flip between costs/benefits, advantages/disadvantages. Please note that you don't always have to give both sides of the debate.
Compare	Demonstrate knowledge and understanding of the similarities and/or differences between two things, methods, features or choices.	Use the link word 'both' to illustrate similarities between two things and 'whereas' to illustrate differences. The points of comparison must be *related*, i.e. not just two random points.
Distinguish	Demonstrate knowledge and understanding of the differences between methods, features or choices.	Treat this question in a similar way to 'Compare' questions. However, *only* differences should be given, i.e. only use 'whereas' to illustrate differences in 'Distinguish' questions.
Justify	Give reasons to support suggestions or courses of action.	Giving a justification is basically like describing an *advantage* of doing something. Don't ever give a *disadvantage* as this isn't justifying.
Explain	Make points that relate cause and effect and/or make the relationships clear.	You can treat answering these questions as making two statements for 1 mark. To gain each mark you need to relate *cause* and *effect*. There are two ways you can do this: 1) Use the link phrases 'this means', 'meaning' and 'which will' to explain the *effect* after giving a *cause*. 2) Use the link phrase 'as' or 'because' to explain the *cause* after giving the *effect* first.

Exam questions

You should practise exam questions containing all of the command words on page vii. A good way to understand the differences between the command words is to tackle similar questions but with different command words. You will be able to see the differences in the content and quantity of writing needed to gain marks for each one.

You will be able to find similar questions with different command words on the SQA website, www.sqa.org.uk. There they have guidance on which questions you can use from the *old* Higher as well as specimen questions from the *new* Higher. There are also exam-style questions at the end of each chapter in this book. You can also study the solutions provided to see how they should be tackled – after attempting them, of course!

You also need to be aware of the wording of each question as this can give you clues about how to answer it. Let's break down an example question to see what it tells us.

Exam-style question practice

Explain methods of external growth. **(4 marks)**

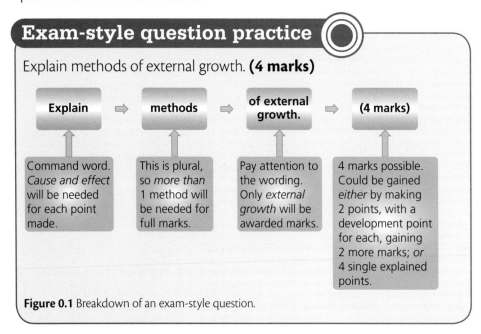

Explain	methods	of external growth.	(4 marks)
Command word. *Cause and effect* will be needed for each point made.	This is plural, so *more than* 1 method will be needed for full marks.	Pay attention to the wording. Only *external growth* will be awarded marks.	4 marks possible. Could be gained *either* by making 2 points, with a development point for each, gaining 2 more marks; *or* 4 single explained points.

Figure 0.1 Breakdown of an exam-style question.

Activity 0.1

Below are five exam-style questions, all on the same straightforward 'introductory' topic that you should cover in the early stages of the course. Attempt all five questions, paying close attention to the command word in each one. Check your answers with a partner or ask your teacher to look over them for you.

1 Describe the features of:
   a) a private limited company
   b) a public limited company. **(4 marks)**
2 Discuss the following types of organisation:
   a) a private limited company
   b) a public limited company. **(4 marks)**
3 Compare the following types of organisation:
   a private limited company and a public limited company. **(4 marks)**
   ⇨

4   Distinguish between the following types of organisation:
    a private limited company and a public limited company. **(4 marks)**

5   Explain why a business would want to:
    a) become a public limited company
    b) remain a private limited company. **(4 marks)**

Coursework assignment

The **coursework assignment** is worth 30 marks (30% of your overall grade) and will be completed by you at school or college and sent to the SQA to be marked. The marks will be awarded as follows:

Element	Maximum marks available
Introduction	2 marks
Research	4 marks
Analysis and interpretation	12 marks
Conclusions and recommendations	10 marks
Collating and reporting findings	2 marks
Total	**30 marks**

Your assignment is to research an organisation of your choice AND a **business issue** of your choice, and produce a **report** of your findings. The organisation can be from any sector of the economy, that is, private, public or third sector. The business issue should be directly related to a topic and/or concept from the Higher Business Management course. This should not be an entire unit but a specific topic. For example if you want to investigate Coca Cola and are particularly interested in marketing, you could choose:

- the pricing strategies of Coca Cola
- the product portfolio of Coca Cola
- the channels of distribution of Coca Cola
- the below-the-line promotions of Coca Cola.

Once you have decided on your organisation and business issue, you then have to plan and gather evidence. You have 6½ hours to do this. Make sure you split the time up appropriately – don't spend too long researching background information on your chosen organisation for the introduction as this section is only worth 2 marks. Once you have completed the planning stage, you will have a final 1½ hours, in class, to complete your report.

Let's take a look at each section.

Introduction (2 marks)

The **introduction** should set the tone of your report.

1 First, you *must* state the organisation you are researching and the business issue you have chosen.

2 You should give some background information on the organisation, for example, a brief history, the product or service they provide, their

target market, the structure of the organisation, and so on. Limit this information to two points only.

3   You should also explain the analytical technique you will be using later in the report.

Research (4 marks)

The **research** section requires you to justify the methods of research you have chosen.

1   You must choose at least two sources of information. These can be gathered via field or desk research. For example:
   ● websites – your chosen business and/or the competition's
   ● review sites – a quick way to access customer opinions
   ● social media – you may have to gather this evidence at home
   ● surveys – you could set up an online survey to ask your classmates questions
   ● personal interviews – perhaps with a customer or an employee if you can
   ● notes from field trips or guest speakers
   ● newspapers/magazines/catalogues – can provide valuable visual evidence.

2   You have to explain why you have chosen these sources – why they were useful to your report.

3   You should also explain the value of each source, for example, the advantages of using the source.

4   *Do not* list everything you found out from your research in this section, this is done later.

Analysis and interpretation (12 marks)

The **analysis and interpretation** section is the main body of your report where you present your findings from your research.

Each analysis and interpretation point you make should relate to evidence from your research. This evidence could be presented as a graph, image or table and can be included as an appendix at the end of your report, signposted in this section. For example, Source 1, Source 2, and so on.

1   Your research evidence should also be analysed using an **analytical technique**. Examples of analytical techniques you could use are:
   ● SWOT analysis
   ● PESTEC analysis
   ● product portfolio (Boston matrix)
   ● ratio analysis

2   Each point you make should *either* link your research evidence to:
   a) your knowledge and understanding of the business issue

OR b) the analytical technique you used.

   In other words *don't* just list your research evidence; you must *add* to each piece of evidence either by linking it to theory or analysing it with one of the techniques above.

Hints & tips

A good way to ensure you analyse your research evidence is to reference or write out a piece of evidence and then write "this shows..." or "it is clear that..." before analysing what it shows or tells you in relation to your topic!

Conclusions and recommendations (10 marks)

This is the final section of your report, woo hoo!

1   You should make **conclusions** based on positives that you have found, so explain the likely benefits of something the organisation does well, based on your evidence.
2   You should also make **recommendations** based on negatives that you have found, so explain what the organisation should change, introduce or do better *and* the benefits of them doing so.

Collating and reporting (2 marks)

You don't have to do anything specific in this section, just ensure that:

- you have used appropriate headings throughout the report
- your report isn't too long; six A4 typed sides plus four sides of research evidence in the appendices is the *most* you should submit
- you have used appropriate display materials, for example, charts, graphs, images.
- you have used business terminology throughout the report.

Hints & tips

Make sure you are awarded the 2 marks for 'collating and reporting' e.g. it is recommended that you use 11pt font size with 1.5 line spacing. You should view them as free marks that will only be lost through lack of care and attention on your part!

Revision tips

There are three things you must do to prepare for the Higher Business Management exam. They are: revise, revise and revise! Sure, a lot of Business Management is common sense and you can write about experiences you have of business. However, the course has its fair share of topics that you won't know before you study the course and won't remember your teacher teaching you either. So, you *have* to revise.

Here are a few things you can do to make your revision effective.

Key terms spreadsheet

Creating and updating a key terms spreadsheet should be an ongoing revision activity that you do throughout your studies. If it is already too late, try creating one during your study leave as you revise each topic.

Activity 0.2

1   Create a table using spreadsheet software, add four columns: Term, Definition, Advantage and Disadvantage.
2   Use the Glossary at the back of your textbook to find out what key terms are used in the course so should be on your list. Try and pick out the ones you know first and define them yourself. Then look up the terms you don't know or can't remember.
3   Revise these terms. Copy down some notes, use the internet to find out some more and then update your spreadsheet. You can sort your spreadsheet alphabetically or you could have a different sheet for each topic. It's up to you.

Questions that give you the fear!

As you revise by tackling exam-style questions – either from this book, the SQA website or from your teacher – there will be questions that you really don't like the look of. In other words, they give you 'the fear'! A revision technique I use with my own students at school is to stop avoiding these questions and actually *embrace* them. You should do this too! The more you practise answering them, the more straightforward and less daunting they will become.

So, flick through the exam-style questions in this book, specimen papers, old past papers, and so on and make a list of the questions that, off the top of your head, you can't think of an answer that would score you *at least half* of the available marks. These are your 'fear' questions. Don't avoid them; revise them. (Chances are the extra time you spend looking at these areas will be all it takes to give you some confidence.) Attempt the question. Don't worry if you can't get full marks; remember, you *were* struggling to get even some or any marks before! Take your answer to your teacher or check it yourself.

It is also especially important to do this, as all questions in the final exam are mandatory so, you never know – the type of questions that give you the fear might just come up!

Mind maps

Mind maps are useful in Higher Business Management as there is so much jargon, theory and terms.

- Ever heard the phrase 'a picture is worth a thousand words'? Including visual representations of the information, as drawings and images, in your revision notes will really help it stick in your mind.
- What is more, by the time you finish the course, you should start to see patterns emerging and the same theory being repeated in different topics – and this will be easy to see when you compare your mind maps.
- You can make a mind map on paper or on a computer – a number of free mind mapping software are available.
- Try making a mind map with a friend. One of you can even record the other drawing your mind map (perhaps after a few practice shots!) and, when you speed it up, it will make a neat revision video. You could even dub commentary over the top.

Make sure you go into that exam ready for it. As an examiner myself, I know when a candidate is prepared – it leaps right off the page when I mark their question paper. Make sure that's how your question paper looks!

Enjoy the course, enjoy your studies and all the very best.

Now, on with the book!

Remember

… passing Higher Business Management is down to you – your hard work, your revision, you paying attention in class. You have to submit the best assignment you possibly can and make sure you answer every question in the exam to the best of your ability – never leave a question blank! But you can do it – there is nothing stopping you!

Chapter 1

Outcome 1.1: Features, Objectives and Structures of Organisations

What you should know

There are three main parts to this outcome. By the end of this outcome you should be able to:

1 **Compare** features of large organisations from different sectors of the economy.
2 **Identify** the objectives of large organisations and **describe** the importance of them.
3 **Describe** the internal structures that large organisations may use and **justify** why they use them.

Remember

*... the difference between **goods** and **services**! Goods are things that you buy that are tangible (you can physically touch them). A service is something you use. They are intangible (you can't physically see or touch them). Both goods and services are known as **products**.*

Sectors of industry

At Higher level Business Management, you need to be aware of **four** sectors of industry:

1 **Primary sector**. This consists of businesses that are involved in exploiting natural resources. Examples include farming, mining and oil drilling.
2 **Secondary sector**. This consists of businesses that are involved in manufacturing and construction, by taking natural resources and turning them into **goods** that can be sold later. Examples include electronics manufacture, car production and house building.
3 **Tertiary sector**. This consists of businesses and organisations that are involved in providing **services** rather than goods. Examples include retail outlets, banks, hotels and hospitals.
4 **Quaternary sector**. This consists of businesses providing information and knowledge-based services, such as:
   ● ICT (information and communication technology)
   ● consultancy (offering advice to businesses)
   ● R&D (research and development).

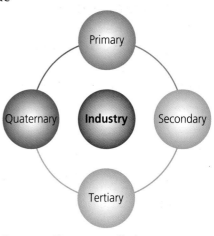

Figure 1.1 The sectors of industry.

Sectors of the economy

There are **three** sectors of the economy:

1 **Private sector**. This consists of businesses that aim primarily to maximise **profits** and includes all profit-making businesses ranging from your local high-street bakery to huge multinational companies such as Ford and Samsung.

2 **Public sector**. This consists of government-owned organisations and agencies which aim to provide a service to society. This sector of the economy includes the NHS, police and state education.

3 **Third sector**. This consists of organisations that have been set up to provide goods or services to benefit others. This sector of the economy includes:
- charities such as Cancer Research and the SSPCA
- voluntary organisations such as golf clubs and Scouts groups
- social enterprises
- democratic enterprises such as co-operatives.

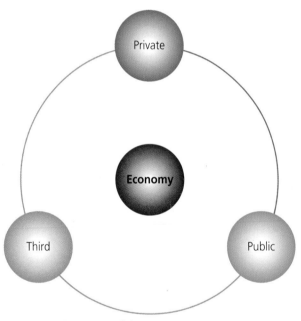

Figure 1.2 The sectors of the economy.

The private sector

Private limited companies

Limited companies get their name because they have **limited liability**. This means that owners' personal possessions are not at risk. If the business gets into debt with creditors, the owners only lose their investment in the company. The owners of a limited company are called **shareholders** as they have one or more share in the business. In other words, they share ownership of the business with others. In a **private limited company (Ltd)** shares are not available to the general public and are sold privately to investors whom the business knows, such as employees.

Private limited companies aim to maximise profits, to grow and perhaps increase market share. They are controlled by a **board of directors** who are managed by a managing director. All limited companies have to produce complex documents called the **Memorandum of Association** and **Articles of Association** that outline the rules of the company, such as shareholders' rights and the responsibilities of the directors.

Table 1.1 Advantages and disadvantages of private limited companies

Advantages	Disadvantages
Owners (shareholders) have limited liability.	Profits have to be split with many shareholders by issuing **dividends**.
Ownership is not lost to outsiders.	A complicated legal process is required to set up the company.
The business usually retains a close and tight-knit, friendly feel with a high level of customer service.	A limited source of capital is available as shares are not sold publicly.
Expertise and business acumen are gained from an experienced board of directors.	Financial statements have to be shared with Companies House (and are therefore made publically available), meaning profits are not kept private.

Public limited companies

Public limited companies (PLC), like private limited companies, are owned by shareholders who have **limited liability**. They are also controlled by a board of directors. However, unlike private limited companies, public limited companies can sell their shares publicly, through the stock market.

You may have heard of the FTSE 100 (Financial Times Stock Exchange). This is a list of the 100 highest valued PLCs in the UK. Their shares are **traded** (bought and sold) on the London stock exchange. The FTSE 100 contains companies such as Vodafone, Tesco and SKY.

PLCs aim to dominate the market, increase market share and increase market value (the total value of all their shares).

WWW

Take a look at Yahoo's finance pages and find out for yourself about the public limited companies on the London Stock Exchange. You will be amazed at the brands you will recognise:

https://uk.finance.yahoo.com

Table 1.2 Advantages and disadvantages of public limited companies

Advantages	Disadvantages
Shareholders have limited liability.	Dividends are shared with many shareholders.
Large amounts of finance can be raised through the public sale of shares.	Control of the business can be lost as anyone can buy shares on the stock market.
It is easy to borrow finance due to a PLC's size and reputation, so less risk for banks.	Annual accounts have to be published.
PLCs can easily dominate the market.	Setting up a PLC is costly and complicated.

Franchise

A **franchise** is a business model that allows businesses to pay a sum of money to own a branch of a well-known, existing business. The main, original business is known as the **franchiser** and the owner of each individual branch is known as a **franchisee**. Some of the best known franchises are McDonald's, Subway, Papa John's and Red Driving School.

The franchiser's main aim is to grow and increase market share and the franchise model allows this. They also aim to maximise profits and, if they are a PLC, increase their market value too. Each franchisee has very little decision-making power over important strategic and tactical decisions (see Chapter 3) as these are made by the main franchiser.

Table 1.3 Advantages and disadvantages of a franchise for the franchiser

Advantages for the *franchiser*	Disadvantages for the *franchiser*
A low risk form of growth as the franchisee invests the majority of the capital.	The reputation of the whole franchise can be tarnished by one poor franchisee.
Receives a percentage of all franchisee's profits each year (known as **royalties**).	Only a share of profits is received rather than all profits as it would be if they owned each branch.

Table 1.4 Advantages and disadvantages of a franchise for the franchisee

Advantages for the *franchisee*	Disadvantages for the *franchisee*
The franchise is a well-known business with an existing customer base.	There is very little autonomy over decisions as the franchiser decides on products, store layout, uniforms, etc.
Industry knowledge and training is provided by the franchiser.	Royalties have to be paid each year.
The franchisee benefits from national advertisements carried out by the franchiser.	There are high initial start-up fees.

WWW

Find out for yourself about the franchise opportunities available in the UK. You can read about the financial costs of becoming a franchisee as well as the franchise package and benefits a franchisee would receive at **www.franchisedirect.co.uk**

Multinationals

A multinational is a business that has operations in more than one country. This could be world-wide retail outlets such as *Asda Walmart* or just retail outlets in one country and a production facility in another. Most multinationals are limited companies. Their head office is usually based in the **home country**.

In recent years it has become easier to operate as a multinational due to the improvement in **infrastructure**, for example, inexpensive air travel, single currencies such as the Euro, and the growth of e-commerce. All of these have helped the world become one big market place; this is known as **globalisation** and it has helped some multinationals become massively successful.

The effects of multinationals on **host countries** are debatable. On one hand, multinationals provide jobs and training and can have a positive effect on local economies. On the other hand, they can exploit low-paid labour, use up natural resources, put local firms out of business and take their profits back to their home country.

Table 1.5 Advantages and disadvantages of multinationals

Advantages	Disadvantages
Wages and raw material costs are lower in host countries.	Language barriers can slow down communication.
Business can avoid legislation in the home country.	Cultural differences can affect production, e.g. 'siestas' in Spain.
Grants can be issued by governments to locate in their country.	Exchange rates can affect purchasing and paying expenses in different countries.
Business can avoid quotas (retraction on amount of imports/exports) and tariffs (taxes on imports/exports) issued by their own governments.	Time differences can hinder communication between head office and branches around the world.

The public sector

Central government

The UK Government provides national services to the citizens of the UK that it would be very difficult to rely on the private sector to provide. For example, defence by the armed forces, healthcare through the NHS and a transport infrastructure through the road network. These are critical services paid for through **taxation**.

The overall control of policy surrounding these organisations is held by elected politicians. Individual departments are controlled by employed citizens, called civil servants. In Scotland, the Scottish Parliament oversees **devolved** services, such as Education and the Police.

All central government organisations aim to provide a quality service.

The public sector also includes any **nationalised** companies. This means private sector businesses that have been bought in part or in full by the government, to stop them from going bust. An example of this was when the UK Government bought shares in Royal Bank of Scotland (RBS) during the recent recession.

The opposite of nationalising is **privatising**, which is selling a public sector organisation to the private sector, for example, when the Royal Mail was floated on the stock market in 2013.

Remember

Many students get confused between the **public sector** and **public limited companies**. They are not the same, in fact, quite the opposite! So why do they both have public in their title? Well, the public sector serves the general public for free and public limited companies can sell shares to the general public.

Local government

Local government in Scotland is split up into local authorities, such as Fife Council, South Lanarkshire Council, Stirling Council and so on. They provide essential services to the public such as schools, refuse collection and street lighting, free of charge.

Top level, **strategic** decision-making is carried out by elected councillors, while the **tactical** decisions and **operational** day-to-day running of individual organisations are in the hands of managers and employees of the council, such as the head teacher of your local state secondary school.

Finance comes from taxation collected by central government, local council tax and local business rates. Some organisations, such as a council-owned leisure centre, also charge for services to fund running costs.

All local government organisations aim to provide a quality service. They don't aim to make profits, however some public sector organisations, such as schools, do aim to stick to their given budget and not overspend.

The third sector

Charities

Charities are set up with the sole purpose of raising money to benefit others. They raise finance through donations, sponsorship and fundraising events. They may also have a **trading arm**. This could be through a retail outlet that trades to raise money, such as a high street Oxfam shop, however any profits they make are given to their cause rather than kept by the owners. There is no individual owner of a charity, instead it is set up as a **trust**. The overall control of the trust is carried out by a **board of trustees**, while some individual outlets or departments can be managed by paid managers who are assisted by **volunteers**.

The main aims and objectives of charities depend on the individual cause at the heart of the organisation. For instance, the SSPCA (Scottish Society for the Prevention of Cruelty to Animals) aims to improve the welfare of animals in Scotland, while UNICEF aims to protect children's rights worldwide.

Table 1.6 Advantages and disadvantages of charities

Advantages	Disadvantages
Charities are exempt from paying some taxes, such as VAT and Corporation Tax.	It can be difficult to compete with the large marketing budgets of organisations within the private sector.
There are low wage costs due to volunteers working for free.	Charities rely heavily on volunteers who may leave for paid work.
Private companies are more willing to donate to and sponsor charities than ever before as it is good 'PR'.	

Voluntary organisations

Voluntary organisations aim to provide a service for their members and the local community, for example, a local sports club such as a golf club or youth football team. They raise finance mostly through membership subscriptions (sometimes known as 'subs'). They are controlled and run by an **elected committee** and helped by volunteers.

Social enterprises

Social enterprises are organisations that aim to make a profit to benefit a specific group or cause, for example, *The Big Issue* is a magazine that aims to help the homeless in the UK.

Unlike non-profit organisations they operate as private sector businesses do, in that they can be owned by one person (sole trader), two to twenty people (partnership) or shareholders in a limited company. Also, similar to the private sector, control can be in the hands of a board of directors or paid managers and finance can come from capital investment or bank loans. However, the main difference between social enterprises and organisations within the private sector is that their profits benefit a social, environmental or cultural cause and not solely the owners of the business.

Table 1.7 Advantages of a social enterprise

Advantages
Social aims can endear a social enterprise to customers.
Good quality employees who believe in the social 'mission' are attracted to the organisation.
They are likely to receive government grants due to their positive impact on society.
'**Asset lock**' means that, should the enterprise be closed down, the sale of any assets and any profits will be used to benefit their cause.

Case study 1.1
Jamie Oliver's Fifteen

Chef, entrepreneur and TV personality, Jamie Oliver has established a reputable London-based restaurant called Fifteen. The business offers young, unemployed people the experience of learning to work in the restaurant industry. In 2002, Jamie opened the first Fifteen restaurant in London, and recruited 15 young apprentices to train alongside a team of 25 professional chefs. He also set up a charity that would receive all the profits from the restaurant, in order to fund the programme.

Jamie said on the business' website that he was 'particularly excited by the social enterprise model whereby a business is driven primarily by social ambition rather than financial gain'. His vision, which took almost ten years to bring to fruition, was to use the magic of food to give unemployed young people a chance to have a better future.

Figure 1.3 Jamie Oliver is a celebrity chef and entrepreneur.

Discussion points

In pairs, groups or on your own, consider:

1 How might society benefit from Jamie Oliver's social enterprise?
2 How can Fifteen and Jamie Oliver's other brands benefit from this social enterprise?

www

Take a look at the social enterprise movement in the UK for yourself at **www.socialenterprise.org.uk**

Democratic enterprises

Increasingly in the EU and USA, democratic enterprises are being developed. All of these businesses share the same objective of generating profit. They differ from private sector businesses in that they aim to make but not necessarily *maximise* profit. Decision-making and profits are shared among members *democratically*. Democratic enterprises are becoming ever more popular with governments which are keen to encourage enterprise and increase wealth in their economy, but which also want their citizens to share in this prosperity.

7

Co-operatives

A good example of a democratic enterprise is a co-operative, whose main aim is to provide a quality service for the benefit of its members and customers. Co-operatives invite their customers and employees to become members, who then share ownership, decision-making and profits (known as 'dividends').

Co-operatives also subscribe to an internationally agreed set of values and principles, which define their ethical approach to business. These values and principles *and* their democratic structure are what distinguishes co-ops from organisations following the social enterprise model.

WWW

Read more about what a co-operative is at
www.uk.coop/what-co-operative

Case study 1.2
The Co-operative Group

The best known **co-operative** in the UK is The Co-operative Group (often called the 'Co-op') who have a range of services including food stores, funeral, insurance and legal services. Customers can become members for just £1 and can have a say in decisions, such as how best to help the local community, as well as sharing in any profits.

The co-operative

Figure 1.4 The Co-operative Group is the largest co-operative in the UK.

Discussion points

In pairs, groups or on your own, consider:

1   Why might it be good for local communities to have organisations such as the Co-operative Group?
2   In what ways do customers benefit from The Co-operative Group?

Activity 1.1

Wow! I'm sure you will agree that the sectors of the economy topic has a lot of information to take in. This is an important topic that many students find difficult. A good way to summarise the information in this topic is by creating a table like the one below. Try it for yourself.

1   Create a table like the one below, either in your notebook, on your computer or even as an A3 poster.

2   Use the previous pages to gather information about all the features of the main types of business organisations to complete your table.

3   Then try it again, but this time without looking at the book. You may be amazed at how much you remember!

	Private Sector				Public Sector		Third Sector	
	Ltd	PLC	Multinational	Franchise	Central govt.	Local govt.	Charities	Social ent.
Ownership								
Control								
Main finance								
Main aims								
Advantages								
Disadvantages								

Key questions 1.1

1 Describe the three sectors of the economy.
2 Describe the four sectors of industry.
3 Outline three features of a PLC.
4 Describe two third-sector organisations.

Essential question 1.1

Compare two features of a PLC with those of a public-sector organisation.

Remember

... to follow the command word (in bold) in the essential questions. This is crucial to meet the standard for each outcome.

Objectives

Maximising profits

Making a **profit** means bringing in more money through the business' core activities, such as selling goods and services, than they spend on purchasing materials and other running costs of the business, such as wages and rent. As a business grows it will aim to **maximise profits** which means making as much profit as possible.

Survival

All private sector businesses and, indeed, third sector businesses aim to **survive**. Survival means avoiding going out of business and having to cease trading. Periods of **economic slowdown** (see Chapter 2), such as a recession, are particularly turbulent times for businesses and many fail, even large PLCs.

Satisficing

Satisficing means aiming for a *satisfactory* or adequate result, rather than the best possible outcome. Most private sector businesses would ideally aim to maximise profits; however, through satisficing, a business could aim only to make a level of profit which is good enough to satisfy the main stakeholders, perhaps making enough profit to cover satisfactory dividends to shareholders.

Provide a quality service

All organisations aim to provide a **quality service** to their customers or members. Private sector businesses aim to do this to encourage customers to return and to gain a good reputation and attract new customers. Public sector organisations do this to satisfy the needs of the community and improve the standards of living in their area, such as a school offering a quality education. Third sector organisations want to provide a quality service to aid those individuals or groups they aim to help.

Increasing market share

Market share is the percentage of total sales in a market that a business has. The business that has the most sales in a market is known as the **market leader**. Businesses aim to improve their products and services to ensure that existing customers return *and* to try to entice their rivals' customers to their business. Market share can be illustrated as a pie chart as shown in Figure 1.5.

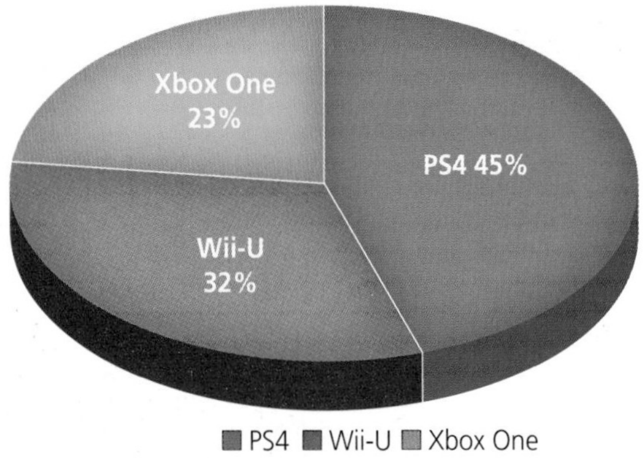

PS4 45% | Wii-U 32% | Xbox One 23%

■ PS4 ■ Wii-U ■ Xbox One

Figure 1.5 The games console market share clearly shows the Sony PS4 as the market leader.

Managerial objectives

Managers within large PLCs or public sector organisations may pursue their own objectives. They may try to achieve objectives which they believe will improve their status within the company, for example, expansion into new markets, or developing new technologies. They may also aim to have many subordinates reporting to them in order to increase their responsibility, and therefore their salary.

> **Hints & tips** ⭐
>
> *Market share is covered in greater detail in National 5.*

Sales maximisation

Similar to managerial objectives above, the objective of sales maximisation can arise due to management aiming to achieve personal goals rather than the aims of the business. For example, to **maximise sales** could mean dropping the selling price of a product; managers, salespeople and even entire branches who are on **commission** for the *number* of sales made, will be less interested in the overall profits of the business and more interested in selling as many units as possible.

Corporate social responsibility

Corporate social responsibility (CSR) refers to organisations aiming to act in an ethical way or in *any* way that benefits either society or the environment.

Methods to ensure good CSR

Ethical and environmental responsibilities (see Chapter 7), for example, avoiding the use of child labour.

Philanthropy (see Chapter 7), for example, donating to charity.

Economical responsibilities, for example, using fair and competitive marketing (see Chapter 6).

Legal responsibilities, for example, abiding by laws that govern businesses.

Advantages of positive CSR

There are a number of key advantages for a business of having positive CSR:
- The business gains a good reputation for its caring nature.
- Customers who agree with the aim are likely to use the business.
- The business can attract high-quality staff who believe in the ethics of the business.
- Society and the environment are kept in good order, which will benefit the business in the long run.

Case study 1.3
Lush

Lush is a huge multinational company that specialises in fresh handmade cosmetics. Despite its size, it is an organisation with positive CSR at its heart. Just take a look at this screenshot from their website.

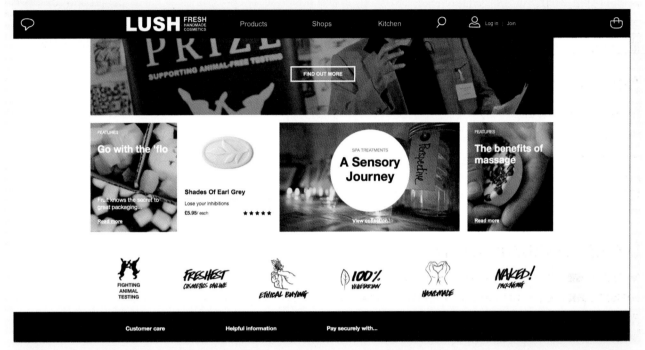

Figure 1.6 Lush website showing their commitment to CSR.

Lush are now renowned for their active campaigns against animal testing. They use fair trade products, encourage recycling and low-waste packaging, and they donate to charity through selling 'Charity Pot', a hand and body lotion.

They have even set up their own charitable fund, called the 'SLush Fund'. Two per cent of the total amount Lush spends on raw materials and packaging is donated to the fund. This money is then used to start sustainable farming and community projects from scratch, some of which produce and process ingredients for their products.

Discussion points

In pairs, groups or on your own, consider:

1   How many examples of good CSR can you spot in the single screenshot?
2   Why should more organisations aim to be as thorough about CSR as Lush?

Growth

After starting up, a successful business will aim to grow. To 'grow' means to make the business larger. Not all organisations will aim to grow. Local government organisations, for example, aim instead to serve the local community; growing is not of interest to them. Some private limited companies like to stay small too, as their customers like the personal touch that bigger franchises and multinationals cannot offer. However, if a business does grow it will realise a number of advantages.

Table 1.8 The advantages of growth

Advantage	Explanation
Reduces the risk of failure	Bigger businesses with more products or branches can spread the risk and avoid 'putting all their eggs in one basket'.
Increases profits	More products to sell or more stores to sell them in will equal more sales, and more profits.
Avoids being taken over	Bigger businesses aim to buy smaller businesses to control their products, outlets and customers. By growing larger, a business can be the 'big fish in the pond' and avoid being eaten themselves.
Removes competition	Bigger businesses can put smaller ones out of business and this can significantly increase the market share of the bigger business.
Economies of scale	Bigger businesses can benefit purely from being so large, for example, ● **Bulk buying**. The more materials a business purchases, the cheaper the unit cost is. Just as when you buy a multipack of crisps, the unit cost (cost per individual bag) is cheaper than when you buy a single bag. ● **Finance**. Finance is easier to obtain from banks and interest is at a lower rate than for smaller businesses. ● **Specialist functions**. Large businesses can afford to have specialist departments (known as 'functions'). For instance having a dedicated marketing department with expert staff will mean promotions will be more effective than those of smaller businesses.

Methods of growth

Internal/Organic growth

This means businesses deciding to grow on their own without getting involved with other organisations. Growing in this way will increase market share without losing control of the business to outsiders. See Table 1.9 for more information about internal/organic growth methods.

Table 1.9 Internal/organic growth methods

Internal/Organic growth method	Description
Launching new products/ services	Businesses can meet the needs of different market segments, especially if they **diversify**, i.e. launch new products into different markets from their current ones or export existing products abroad.
Opening new branches or expanding existing branches	A business can reach new markets by opening up in new locations. It can also expand existing premises to cater for more products/staff and more customers, make more sales.
Introducing e-commerce	By selling online, a business can trade 24/7 to a global market.
Hiring more staff	Increasing the number of staff will improve the business' ability to make sales, make better decisions and develop more products.
Increasing production capacity	Businesses can invest in new **capital** and technology to make more products themselves.

Integration

Integration means two businesses becoming one. There are two ways that this can happen.

1 **Takeover**. Here, one business (usually a larger business) buys another (usually smaller) business. This can often be hostile and comes as a result of the smaller business struggling financially and the larger business exploiting the situation. Takeovers (also known as **acquisitions**) sometimes result in the smaller business' stores or outlets taking the name of the larger one, as was the case when

Spanish bank Santander took over Abbey National. Sometimes the larger company just wants to add another product or service to its portfolio, for example, when Google bought YouTube.

Table 1.10 Advantages and disadvantages of takeovers

Advantages	Disadvantages
The buying business gains the market share and resources of the taken-over business.	Integration can lead to job losses in the taken-over business as the buying business wants its own management and employees.
Risk of failure can be spread.	If the buying business moves the headquarters or production to its home country/area, this can have a bad effect on the taken-over business' local economy.
Economies of scale can be achieved.	Integration can be bad for customers as less competition means higher prices.
Competition is reduced, which will increase sales.	A change of name can put off loyal customers of the taken-over business.
	It can be expensive to acquire another business.

2 **Merger**. This means two businesses agreeing to join forces and become one organisation. This is often friendlier than a takeover and can result in a new name and logo for the new, merged organisation.

Table 1.11 Advantages and disadvantages of mergers

Advantages	Disadvantages
Market share and resources are shared, which can spread risk of failure and increase profits.	Customers may dislike the changes a merger may bring e.g. new logo, new name etc … as the familiarity of the previous businesses are lost.
Economies of scale can be achieved.	Marketing campaigns to inform customers of changes can be expensive.
Each business can bring different areas of expertise to the merger.	Can be bad for customers as less competition will mean higher prices.
Unlike a takeover, jobs are more likely to be spared in both businesses.	
Can overcome barriers to entering a market, such as strong competition.	

Case study 1.4
Disney–Pixar

Up until the launch of *Cars*, Disney had used Pixar, experts in computer animation, to produce their CGI (computer generated imagery) movies. This is known as **outsourcing** and is covered later in the chapter. Then, rather than Disney paying for Pixar to work with them on projects, a merger was suggested and the two businesses became one. Unlike some takeovers, however, you can clearly see the identities of the two original businesses have been kept intact in the images shown.

Discussion points

In pairs, groups or on your own, consider:

1 Why do you think Disney and Pixar merged?
2 Suggest the benefits of keeping the original names and logos in the new company name.

Case Study 1.5

Aviva

Some mergers result in a complete overhaul of the brand, known as **rebranding**. This was the case when insurance companies Norwich Union and CGU merged. They wanted a completely new name as it was felt that using the name of the UK town 'Norwich' in the name would hinder the new company from reaching world-wide markets. Search 'Norwich Union' and 'CGU' on the internet and take a look at their respective logos – then do the same for 'Aviva'. You can clearly see that homage is paid to the two previous businesses in the new Aviva logo.

Discussion points

In pairs, groups or on your own, consider:

1   What are the benefits of this merger and complete rebrand?
2   Might there be any drawbacks of the complete rebranding following the merger?

Any takeover or merger is an example of a type of integration.

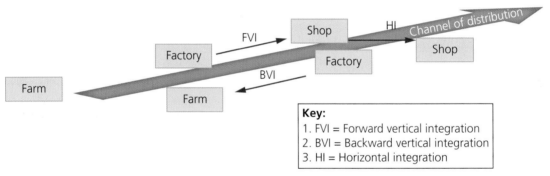

Figure 1.7 Types of integration.

Horizontal integration

Horizontal integration occurs when two businesses from the *same* sector of industry become one business. This could be two dairy farms **merging** (primary sector) or one bank **taking over** another bank (tertiary sector).

Table 1.12 Advantages and disadvantages of horizontal integration

Advantages	Disadvantages
The new, larger business can dominate the market as competition will be vastly reduced.	The merger/takeover may breach EU competition rules.
The new business can benefit from economies of scale, e.g. buying in bulk to reduce prices.	Quality may suffer due to lack of competition.
Due to reduced competition, the new larger business can raise prices, increasing profits.	Customers may have to pay higher prices for the same goods.

Forward vertical integration

Vertical integration occurs when two businesses from *different* sectors of industry become one business.

Forward vertical integration is when a business takes over or merges with a business in a *later* sector of industry, often a distributor. An example would be a manufacturer of mobile phones, such as HTC taking over a mobile phone shop, such as Carphone Warehouse.

Normally a secondary business (for example, a mobile phone manufacturer) would sell goods to a tertiary business (for example, a mobile phone shop) at trade price, allowing the tertiary business to add on a margin of profit to the retail price they sell the product at. After taking over a tertiary business, the secondary business is able to sell their product directly to customers for the more expensive retail price, therefore **adding value** to their selling price and increasing profits.

Backward vertical integration

Backward vertical integration is when a business takes over or merges with a business in an *earlier* sector of industry, in other words they take over their supplier. An example would be a coffee company, such as Starbucks taking over a coffee bean plantation.

Remember

… the primary sector is the *start* of a product being created and the tertiary sector is the *end*, where consumers buy goods. So:

☞ *forward* vertical integration: moving closer *to* the consumer.

☞ *backward* vertical integration: moving *back* towards the raw materials.

Table 1.13 The different advantages and shared disadvantages of forward vertical and backward vertical integration.

Advantages of forward vertical integration	• The business can control supply of their products and could decide to not supply to competition.
	• Can increase profits by 'cutting out the middle man'.
Advantages of backward vertical integration	• Guaranteed and timely supply of stock.
	• No need to pay a supplier their marked-up prices so stock is cheaper.
	• Quality of supplies can be strictly controlled.
Disadvantages of both backward vertical and forward vertical integration	• Company may be incapable of managing new activities efficiently, meaning higher costs.
	• Focusing on new activities can adversely affect core activities.
	• Monopolising markets may have legal repercussions.

Conglomerate integration

Conglomerate integration occurs when businesses in different markets join together. In other words, a merger of businesses whose activities are totally unrelated. Businesses do this primarily to spread the risk of failure, but they will also, of course, increase their chances of maximising profits by having more and varied products and services for sale.

Table 1.14 Advantages and disadvantages of conglomerate integration

Advantages	Disadvantages
The business can spread risk. If one market fails, the losses can be compensated for by profits in another.	One business may take on another in a market they know nothing about and this may cause the new business to fail.
It can overcome seasonal fluctuations in their markets and have more consistent year-round sales.	Having too many products across different markets can cause the company to lose focus on core activities, impacting on other products.
The business is larger and therefore more financially secure.	The business may become too large and inefficient to manage.
The buyer acquires the assets of the other company.	
The business gains the customers and sales of the acquired business.	

Case study 1.6
Proctor & Gamble

Proctor & Gamble (P&G) is the world's largest consumer goods conglomerate. You may never have heard of P&G but you will have heard of many of their brands! They include Ariel, Duracell, Pantene Pro V, Oral B, Olay, Gillette and many, many more! P&G, like most conglomerates, managed to get so huge by taking over or merging with lots of other businesses over a number of years. Gillette is one of their most recent acquisitions and is a perfect example of conglomerate integration.

Figure 1.8 A range of P&G's products.

Before the merger, P&G's product portfolio largely omitted the male grooming market and Gillette was the market leader. By taking over Gillette, P&G overcame a tough barrier to entering the market (that is Gillette's large market share), gained their brand name and, of course, all of their customers!

Discussion points

In pairs, groups or on your own, consider:

1   What might the benefits be to P&G of having so many brands in so many markets?
2   Why do you think P&G bought Gillette?

Take a look at the Proctor & Gamble website and see their large and varied product portfolio for yourself: **www.pg.com**

1 On your own or in pairs, identify or find out using the internet which type of integration the following recent examples are:

   a) Amazon taking over Lovefilm
   b) Coca Cola buying Innocent smoothies
   c) Apple buying up various processor-chip manufacturers
   d) Universal buying a chain of cinemas
   e) Thomson merging with First Choice
   f) Volkswagen taking over Porsche
   g) Virgin taking over Random House
   h) L'Oreal buying The Body Shop
   i) Google buying a wind farm.

2 a) Using the internet or the business sections of a quality newspaper, find out some examples of integration of your own.
   b) Ask your teacher or lecturer to check if you have correctly identified the types of integration.
   c) Present your findings as a poster, showing clearly the old logos becoming the new logos and annotating with information about the type of integration, advantages, disadvantages, and so on.

Other methods of growth

Outsourcing

Outsourcing, also known as **contracting-out**, is when an organisation arranges for another organisation to carry out certain activities for them, instead of doing it themselves. A business could outsource their administration, IT work, printing, legal services, marketing or accountancy. Your school may outsource its catering to a specialist catering company. An organisation will generally do this to concentrate on **core activities**.

Table 1.15 Advantages and disadvantages of outsourcing

Advantages	Disadvantages
Outsourcing allows the business to concentrate on doing what they are good at, rather than getting bogged down with additional services.	The business will have less control over outsourced work so quality may fall.
Less labour and equipment is required for outsourced activities, for example, outsourcing printing saves on printers and reprographics staff.	Communication between the businesses needs to be very clear to make sure exact specifications are met.
There should be high-quality work from the outsourced business as it should have greater expertise and specialist equipment.	The business may have to share sensitive information with the outsourced business that could get into the hands of competitors.
The outsourced business may provide the service cheaper than an in-house department could as they can benefit from economies of scale, doing the same work for many other businesses.	Outsourcing could be more expensive than in house as specialists and expertise come at a price.
The business is able to use the service when it is required, so saving costs on idle staff and machinery.	

De-merger

A **de-merger** occurs when a single business splits into two or more separate components. The de-merged components are still owned by the same organisation as before, however they are managed independently of each other.

Table 1.16 Advantages and disadvantages of de-mergers

Advantages	Disadvantages
Each new 'component' can concentrate on its own core activities and grow as a result.	Customers may be put off by the de-merger and abandon the businesses altogether.
Each new component has the best chance to operate efficiently.	There are significant financial costs involved, for example, in re-branding shop fronts, marketing campaigns to inform customers of the change, and so on.
De-merged components can be **divested** which can meet competition regulations, set by the EU.	

Case study 1.7
Lloyds TSB

In 2013 Lloyds TSB – an organisation that existed due to a previous merger in 1995 of Lloyds Bank and TSB – announced that they were splitting into two separate banks: Lloyds Bank and TSB. This came after the EU, under new competition rules, judged in 2009 that greater competition was to be created within the UK banking industry. The advantages of this for customers include better services and more attractive interest rates.

After the initial **de-merger** in 2013, in 2014 Lloyds Banking Group **divested** TSB when it was sold on the stock market. Lloyds Bank and TSB now have an opportunity to focus on more specific products that will respond to the needs of the customers in the target markets they identify. An example of this is TSB stated commitment to 'local banking' whereby each new branch will focus on 'local customers, local businesses and local communities' and money belonging to local communities stays in local communities in the UK.

Discussion points

In pairs, groups or on your own, consider:

1 Why do you think the EU judged that Lloyds Banking Group had to de-merge?
2 Using the context of the case study distinguish between the terms de-merger and divestment.
3 Suggest advantages for customers of more choice in the market.

Divestment

Divestment is selling off part of an organisation, such as a subsidiary company or one of the company's brands. An organisation may divest because it wishes to concentrate on other, more profitable areas of the business, focus on a specific target market or simply to cash in on selling part of the organisation. A previously de-merged component that is then sold off is an example of divestment.

Remember

... divestment is the opposite of investment. In other words, selling part of the business rather than buying a new part of the business.

Case study 1.8

Pringles

Remember Proctor & Gamble, the large conglomerate responsible for many famous household brands? Well, as you would expect for such a large company, as well as taking over and merging with many businesses throughout the years, they have also **divested** too. P&G had only one food brand in its portfolio, Pringles crisps. In 2012, they divested the brand and sold it to Kellogg's. So why would they divest such a profitable and famous brand?

- They received a *huge* sum of money, £2.75 billion to be exact!
- They decided to concentrate on their 'core activities', such as domestic cleaning, beauty and grooming.
- They could invest the profits from the sale of Pringles into their other markets.

Discussion points

In pairs, groups or on your own:

1. Can you think of any reasons why P&G should have held on to Pringles?
2. Explain, in the context of P&G divesting Pringles, what is meant by 'concentrating on core activities'.

Asset stripping

This is taking over another company with intent to sell off its assets for a profit. The individual assets of the organisation, such as factories, retail spaces or fleet, may be more valuable than the organisation as a whole. Asset stripping can cause the buyers to gain a bad reputation as it often happens after they buy another business through a hostile takeover, with the profitable remains of the business being sold off, bit by bit, and the non-profitable areas being closed down.

Key questions 1.2

1. Describe the term 'corporate social responsibility'.
2. Describe the following methods of external growth
   a) Merger
   b) De-merger
   c) Divestment
3. Describe two advantages of growth for a business.

Essential questions 1.2 ?

1 **Identify** two objectives a PLC would have.
2 **Justify** the importance of the objectives you identified above.

Internal structures of organisations

Management structures

Organisations are known as organisations because they are, well, *organised*! Each organisation can use a variety of different methods to organise and group its staff and resources in a way that suits it best. One way in which they can do this is through the main **structure** of the organisation.

Tall structure

Most organisations have a **hierarchy**. This means positions within the organisation with different levels of authority and responsibility; those with the least amount of authority and responsibility at the bottom of the organisation and those with the most at the top. Commands flow down from the decision-makers at the top of the organisation to the workers at the bottom. This is known as the **chain of command**. A tall structure has many levels of management and resembles a large pyramid. This type of structure suits large organisations with many specialised departments.

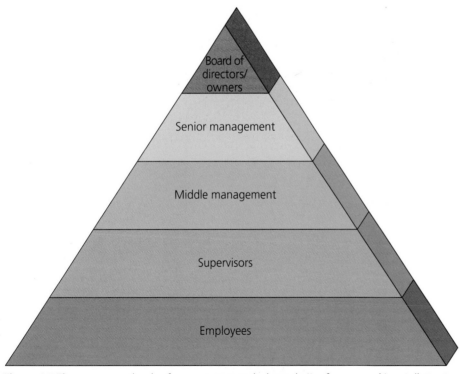

Figure 1.9 There are many levels of management and a long chain of command in a *tall structure.*

Table 1.17 Advantages and disadvantages of a tall structure

Advantages	Disadvantages
Each staff member knows their role and who to report to.	Communications take time to flow down though the levels, which slows down decision-making.
With many levels come many promotion opportunities which can motivate staff.	The organisation can be slow to react to changes in the market.
There is a **narrow span of control** which means: ● managers have more time for planning, supervision and decision-making ● managers can support subordinates.	The **narrow span of control** means: ● managers supervise work more closely, which can put staff under pressure ● managers have fewer staff to share ideas with.

Flat structure

A **flat structure** is also a pyramid-shaped structure and, like a tall structure, commands flow from top to bottom. However, a flat structure has fewer levels of management and a shorter chain of command than a tall structure. This type of structure suits small- to medium-sized organisations.

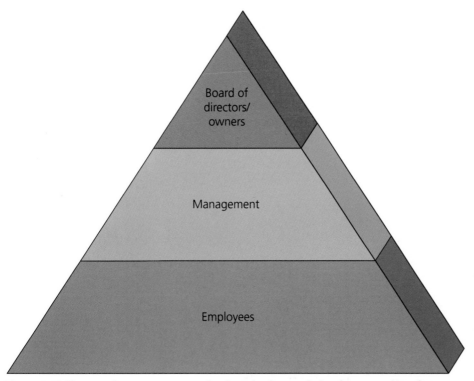

Figure 1.10 There are fewer management levels and a shorter chain of command in a flat structure.

Table 1.18 Advantages and disadvantages of a flat structure

Advantages	Disadvantages
Information can be communicated quickly between levels.	Fewer levels means fewer promotion opportunities so quality staff may leave to gain promotion in larger organisations.
The organisation can respond quickly to external (PESTEC) factors, such as competition.	As there are less management levels, staff may be delegated more tasks, which could put them under pressure.
There is a **wide span of control** which means: ● managers have to delegate tasks to staff which can raise morale as staff feel trusted ● staff are empowered to make decisions themselves.	The **wide span of control** means: ● managers' time is at a premium which can lead to snap decisions ● less time for planning ● subordinates may have no one to seek help from.

Delayering

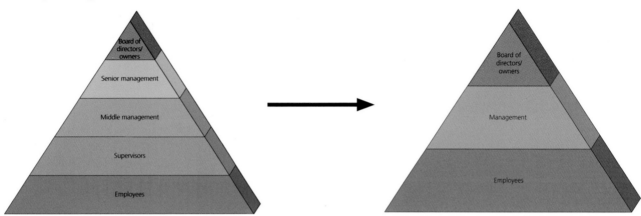

Figure 1.11 An example of delayering.

Removing one or more levels of management from a tall structure, to make it *flatter*, is known as **delayering**.

Table 1.19 Advantages and disadvantages of delayering

Advantages	Disadvantages
Money is saved on paying the salaries of the management level that is removed.	There are fewer promotion opportunities for staff.
Quicker decision-making and communication are possible as there is a shorter chain of command.	Redundancy payments will cost the organisation a significant amount of money.
The organisation can be more responsive to changes in the market as there are fewer levels for information to pass through up to the decision makers.	The organisation will lose key members of staff in the restructure.
There is a wider span of control (see Table 1.18).	

Activity 1.3

1 On your own or in pairs, draw out the structure of your school or college in the form of an organisation chart.
2 Annotate the chart with the key terms listed above such as span of control, chain of command, lateral relationship, and so on.

Hints & tips ⭐

Use these key terms when discussing structures:

✓ **Chain of command:** *The flowing of information and decisions through an organisation.*
✓ **Superior:** *Someone of a higher rank in the organisation.*
✓ **Subordinate:** *Someone of a lower rank in the organisation*
✓ **Line relationship:** *The relationship between a superior and a subordinate.*
✓ **Lateral relationship:** *The relationship between two employees on the same management level.*
✓ **Functional relationship:** *The relationship between two departments.*
✓ **Staff relationship:** *An advisory role, for example between an IT specialist and other staff members.*
✓ **Authority:** *The power to make decisions and to command subordinates.*
✓ **Delegate:** *To pass management tasks onto subordinates.*
✓ **Span of control:** *The number of subordinates working under a superior.*
✓ **Empowerment:** *Staff being given decision-making power.*

Centralised management

Decision-making and control is kept at the very top level of a **centralised** organisation. In organisations with many branches this means important decision-making being retained within head office and the senior management, directors or owners that work there.

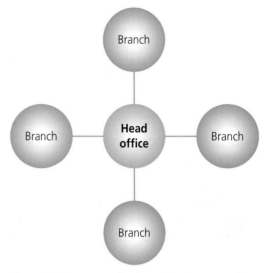

Figure 1.12 In a centralised organisation, control is kept in the centre at the very top level.

Table 1.20 Advantages and disadvantages of a centralised management

Advantages	Disadvantages
A high degree of corporate identity and strategy exists as decisions are made for the whole organisation.	Less responsibility is given to subordinates which can result in demotivated staff.
Procedures are standardised which ensures consistency.	Decisions will not reflect the needs of local markets.
There is low risk of important information leaking from branches or departments.	The organisation will react slowly to external (PESTEC) factors, such as the competition improving their product range.

Decentralised management

Decision-making and control is delegated to individual branches or departments in decentralised organisations. This type of structure is best used in retail chains that need to respond to the needs of their local markets, such as supermarkets. While the overall strategy of an organisation such as Tesco will still be centralised, many decisions will be decentralised, such as buying and selling local products and advertising in the local area.

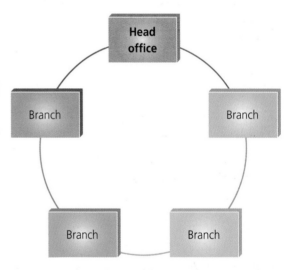

Figure 1.13 In a decentralised organisation, some control is delegated to branches.

Table 1.21 Advantages and disadvantages of decentralised management

Advantages	Disadvantages
The business reacts quickly to changing external (PESTEC) factors.	The organisation can lose an overall corporate image if each department/branch is operating differently.
Decisions are made quickly as local managers don't need to consult senior managers before implementing decisions.	Local branches could start to compete with each other if they are allowed to make key decisions.
More subordinates are empowered which encourages creativity.	
Senior management at head office are relieved of the burden of constant decision-making.	

Matrix structure

A matrix structure involves an organisation being arranged into temporary project teams to carry out a particular task, such as developing a new product or service, or a large-scale construction operation. Teams are made up of employees from different functional areas: marketing, finance, operations, R&D, and so on. Each staff member will have two managers, one will be the manager of their functional area, such as marketing or finance, and the other will be their project manager.

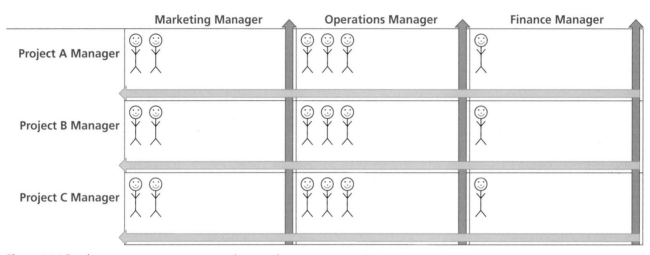

Figure 1.14 Employees report to two managers in a matrix structure.

Table 1.22 Advantages and disadvantages of a matrix structure

Advantages	Disadvantages
Each team has specialised staff from all functional areas.	Many managers across all project teams will mean high wage costs.
Complex problems can be solved.	Duplication of resources such as administration staff and equipment.
Staff can use their expertise and as such have job satisfaction and motivation.	Staff can be confused as to who to report to.

Entrepreneurial structure

This is a structure used primarily by small organisations. Usually they have one main decision-maker, the owner themselves. Of course, other staff can have some input but generally they are rarely consulted and final decisions are made by the owner.

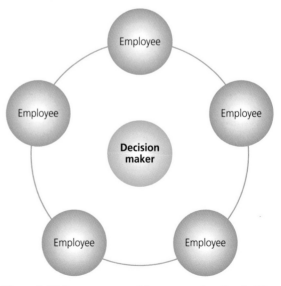

Figure 1.15 An entrepreneurial structure, showing decision-making at the core of the organisation.

Table 1.23 Advantages and disadvantages of an entrepreneurial structure

Advantages	Disadvantages
Decisions are made quickly as there is little consultation.	This structure can create a heavy workload for the main decision maker.
Staff know who they need to report to.	If the owner is busy or not available, key decisions can't be made.
	Other staff don't get a chance to show initiative, stifling creativity and possibly demotivating some staff.

Organisational groupings

As well as using a **management structure** such as tall, flat or entrepreneurial, an organisation can structure themselves through the use of **groupings**.

Functional grouping

This involves grouping an organisation into departments called functional areas, based on skills and expertise. The main functional areas of most organisations are marketing, finance, operations and human resources. These main functional areas can be supported by administration and IT departments. Very small organisations do not have sufficient manpower to be able to group their staff in this way.

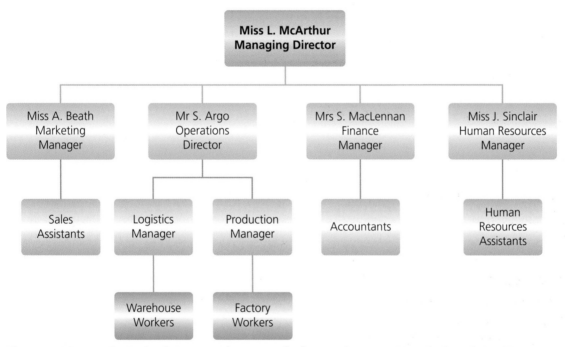

Figure 1.16 An organisation is split into specialist areas in the functional grouping. Note the line relationships between subordinates and superiors – this illustrates chain of command.

Table 1.24 Advantages and disadvantages of functional grouping

Advantages	Disadvantages
Staff with similar skills and expertise are together, allowing for specialisation, i.e. each department becomes excellent at what it does.	The organisation can become too large to manage if functional departments grow rapidly.
Staff know who to report to and can get guidance from more experienced staff in their area of expertise.	Functional grouping is often coupled with a centralised management structure so communication can take a while to filter through to functional departments, causing slow reactions to external (PESTEC) factors.
	Functional departments can be more interested in their own objectives rather than the organisation's objectives as a whole.

Location grouping

This is grouping an organisation into geographical divisions. Each division will operate to serve customers in a particular location. Large organisations, such as multinational businesses, might have a Glasgow office, a London office and a San Francisco office, for example.

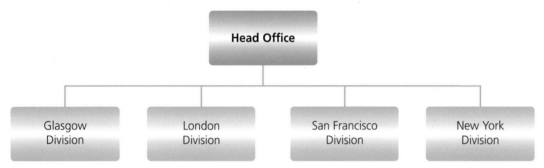

Figure 1.17 Location/Geographical grouping.

Table 1.25 Advantages and disadvantages of location grouping

Advantages	Disadvantages
Each division can meet the needs of its local market, e.g. different tastes or fashions in different areas or countries.	Duplication of resources, such as administration staff or computer equipment, across each group is inefficient.
The business can react to changing external (PESTEC) factors quickly.	Divisions may compete against each other and forget the overall objectives of the organisation as a whole.
It is easy to identify a failing 'area' and hold regional managers accountable.	

Most organisations have both a management structure and a grouping. Figure 1.17 is a diagram of the location grouping and also an example of a centralised management structure. Look at the Product/Service grouping diagram (Figure 1.18). It is also an example of a decentralised structure.

Product/Service grouping

This is grouping an organisation into divisions that deal with different products or services. This is suitable for large conglomerate organisations such as P&G or Virgin. Virgin, for example, has different groups for Virgin Money, Virgin Atlantic, Virgin Media, etc.

Figure 1.18 Virgin grouping.

Table 1.26 Advantages and disadvantages of product/service grouping

Advantages	Disadvantages
The business can react to changing external (PESTEC) factors that affect each particular group's market quickly.	Duplication of resources can occur.
It is easy for management to identify struggling products/services.	A new group needs to be set up every time the business launches a new product – meaning more staff, equipment and premises costs.

Technology Grouping

This is similar to a product/service grouping but involves businesses organising its activities according to the technology or production processes used.

Table 1.27 Advantages and disadvantages of technology grouping

Advantages	Disadvantages
High degree of specialisation can occur in production.	High degree of specialised training is required.
Problems in the production process can be easily identified.	Only an option for very large businesses with different production processes.
Capital intensive - which can reduce wage costs.	Capital intensive – which is expensive.

Customer grouping

This involves grouping the organisation's resources into divisions that each deal with a different type of customer. For example, a business might have a division for retail customers, wholesale customers and online customers.

Figure 1.19 Customer grouping.

Table 1.28 Advantages and disadvantages of customer grouping

Advantages	Disadvantages
Each group can tailor its product or service to its own type of customer.	Duplication of resources can occur.
Customer loyalty can build up due to the high level of personal service that can be achieved.	This is only suitable for large businesses, with many customer types/segments that are of sufficient size. It is inefficient to offer a group for a small customer segment.

Downsizing

This involves an organisation either closing an unprofitable division, such as a location group, altogether or merging two divisions together.

Table 1.29 Advantages and disadvantages of downsizing

Advantages	Disadvantages
This can cut the costs of wages and rent.	Valuable skills and knowledge are lost when redundancies are made.
The business is 'leaner' (more efficient) and can become more competitive.	Remaining staff feel vulnerable and are demotivated.

Key questions 1.3

1 Describe the term 'chain of command'.
2 Discuss the advantages and disadvantages of a matrix structure.
3 Compare a tall management structure with a flat management structure.

Essential questions 1.3

1 **Describe** two internal structures (management structures or groupings) that a business could use.
2 **Justify** the use of the structures you described above.

Exam-style questions practice – Chapter 1

1 Compare the features of a public limited company (PLC) with those of a private limited company (Ltd). **(3 marks)**
2 Describe the advantages of setting up an organisation as a social enterprise. **(4 marks)**
3 Discuss the use of franchising for the franchiser. **(4 marks)**
4 Describe the features of a multinational organisation. **(3 marks)**
5 Explain methods of internal (organic) growth that an organisation can use. **(5 marks)**
6 Discuss the use of outsourcing. **(6 marks)**
7 Describe what is meant by 'market share'. **(2 marks)**
8 Explain the benefits of the matrix structure. **(3 marks)**
9 Distinguish between a decentralised management structure and a centralised management structure. **(3 marks)**
10 Explain the advantages and disadvantages of grouping by location. **(4 marks)**

Remember

... to follow the command word in each exam question! This is the first word in the question and commands you how you should structure your answer.

Chapter 2

Outcome 1.2: Factors Impacting on Business

Internal factors

Internal factors are the different situations that impact on the success of an organisation which arise from *inside* the organisation. Organisations are able to control internal factors.

The availability of finance

All organisations need finance in order to achieve their objectives. The following are possible situations that may arise due to a lack of finance within the organisation:

- The organisation may not be able to implement decisions and take the courses of action it wishes to, such as expanding the business by **developing new products** or offering **wage rises** to motivate staff.
- The organisation may have to take drastic action to cut costs, such as making staff redundancies (**downsizing**) or removing a layer of management (**delayering**).

Human resources

Human resources are the staff in an organisation. 'Staff' means both **managers** *and* **employees**.

Managers can impact on an organisation in the following ways:

1 **Level of risk** – sometimes managers go for the 'safe' option which won't necessarily meet the objectives of the business, such as maximising profits. On the other hand, some managers take too much risk and, when things go wrong, put an organisation into financial difficulties.

2 **Experience and expertise** – a good manager can lead and motivate a team to success, while a bad manager can cause low morale, a high turnover of staff and a drop in productivity.

Employees can impact on an organisation in the following ways:

1 **Training** – a well-trained employee fulfils their role efficiently and is an asset to the company; a badly trained one can be incapable of performing basic functions, such as interacting with customers, and are detrimental to the organisation.

2 **Morale** – employee morale needs to be high as if morale is low it could impact on the performance levels of staff, increase staff absenteeism or worse, lead to industrial action such as a strike.

3 **Experience** – employees need to have experience of doing the job in order to develop the skills and expertise to carry out their jobs effectively.

Technology

An organisation's *existing* technology must be modern and fit for 21st century business. If it is not, the organisation will be left behind by its competitors. The following are just some uses of technology that an organisation should be utilising to remain competitive. More specific uses of technology are covered throughout this book.

- **E-commerce** can be used to sell online via websites. Businesses that do not utilise e-commerce are missing out on a global market and 24/7 sales.
- **Apps** can be used to give businesses a presence on mobile technologies such as smartphones and tablets. This keeps businesses up to date and allows them to meet current customer expectations to be able to find information about and interact with organisations at their fingertips.
- **Email** is used in many organisations to improve the speed of communication and save paper on memos and letters. On the other hand, email is very impersonal and can lead to staff relationships breaking down.

Corporate culture

Corporate culture is the set of values, beliefs and customs that is shared by all people in an organisation. Methods used to develop corporate culture include:

- **Company values** – These need to be developed by the founder as values are hard to 'adopt' years down the line. Examples include having a strong corporate social responsibility (CSR) policy. This can be outlined to stakeholders through a mission statement such as *Ben and Jerry's* mission statement (see Chapter 3).
- **Corporate colours** – Corporate colours give organisations and their staff a strong corporate identity. A good example of this is Easyjet's 'orange' culture. Uniforms, planes, hotels and even their offices are bedecked in their famous orange colour! Colours also help customers recognise the organisation easily.
- **Office layout** – An open-plan office layout can encourage a relaxed atmosphere in an organisation. It can also encourage better communication and idea sharing among staff. Some modern technology companies such as Facebook and Google have very relaxed office environments that include free cafés, sofas and beanbags for staff to sit on, and even sleep pods for staff to have a nap at work!
- **Uniformity of layout** – Ever been to a McDonalds abroad? Exactly the same as in the UK, isn't it? Uniformity of premises such as offices, shops and restaurants makes it easier for staff to transfer between branches and encourages customers to feel at ease, no matter what branch they are in.

- **Language and jargon** – An organisation can invent its own quirky words and phrases that help give employees a sense of belonging and appeal to customers looking to buy from a business that is a bit different. For example, Disneyland theme parks call their staff 'actors' and their customers 'the audience', and Innocent, the smoothie brand, have a very original approach to the language on their packaging.
- **Symbols, slogans and mottos** – The use of brand logos help give organisations identity that both customers and staff easily recognise. Also, the use of slogans and mottos can help reinforce business objectives to staff. For example, Honda's motto 'The Power of Dreams' sums up to designers and production staff that they are a forward-thinking business that designs and produces cutting edge products for customers.
- **Rituals** – Some UK organisations have 'dress-down Fridays' to help relax their staff and break down the barriers that uniforms or office attire can create. Some American businesses have Friday afternoon barbecues for employees to get together and chat informally. Some Japanese companies even meet together in the morning to exercise and chant company songs. Similarly, Southwest Airlines' cabin crew sing the safety instructions and their pilots tell jokes over the intercom!
- **Stories** – Stories of past important events in an organisation's life can help new staff become familiar with the expectations and direction of the organisation. For example, at Proctor & Gamble legend has it that one of their staff members was out shopping and saw an entire shelf of one of their products that was faulty. To save the company embarrassment he bought the shop's entire stock of the product. He was, of course, reimbursed by P&G and applauded for his commitment to ensuring good **quality** (see Chapter 7) in the business.
- **Reward culture** – Many employees respond well to financial incentives such as bonuses, commission and pay rises. Others like the recognition and status of 'employee of the month' awards and promotions.
- **Flexible working arrangements** – An organisation can utilise flexible working arrangements such as flexitime or teleworking (see Chapter 4). This can create a culture of trust and empowerment.

Case study 2.1

Facebook

Most people are aware of the culture at large technology companies such as Google and Facebook from movies such as *The Internship* and *The Social Network*, which portray some of the aspects of modern office culture. The image shows the inside of one of Facebook's offices, complete with coffee shop, comfortable seating and TV. Facebook has a *very* flat organisational structure and employees aren't told what to do. Instead, they are empowered to make their own decisions and start their own projects. There is a very relaxed working environment. Employees can wear casual clothes and start ⇨

and finish when they want, to suit the employee's own preferences. Jobs at Facebook are stressful and some employees work better after a long lie in and work late into the evening. They can work from home, in one of the comfortable areas in the office, in 'third spaces' nearby or at their desk.

Discussion points

In pairs, groups or on your own, consider:

1 What elements of Facebook's corporate culture are evident in the example above?
2 What will be the advantages of Facebook's culture for:
   - employees
   - management?
3 Which elements of Facebook's culture would you like/dislike when you get a job and why?

Table 2.1 Advantages and disadvantages of strong corporate culture

Advantages	Disadvantages
Flexible working arrangements mean staff work when and where they are most productive.	Culture is hard to introduce unless it starts from the founders.
Employees feel part of the organisation through the use of uniforms, jargon, and so on.	Staff have to be made aware of changes to culture and if they aren't they may resist change.
Customers gain a sense of a quality product/service.	Modern office cultures can leave some employees physically and socially distant from others, demotivating them.
Rituals create a relaxed ethos and can improve employee relations.	Some cultures can be seen as a 'bribe' to get staff on board.
Employee loyalty is increased as they are happy in their jobs and feel a sense of belonging to the business.	Management can lose focus and control if a culture is too 'loose'.
High-quality new staff are attracted to the business as they like the idea of working in the culture.	
A relaxed working environment, empowerment and a flat hierarchy can motivate staff.	

Key questions 2.1

1 Describe the ways two different members of staff can impact on an organisation.
2 Describe three ways technology can benefit a business.
3 Describe the term 'corporate culture'.
4 Describe four methods of developing corporate culture.

Essential question 2.1 ?

Explain the impact of two internal factors on a large organisation.

External factors

External factors are the different situations that impact on the success of an organisation that arise *outside* the organisation. The organisation can't control external factors.

Political factors

Political factors affecting organisations arise from decisions made and actions taken by the government, either at a local or national level. This can be changes in laws and legislation, or alterations to a government's **fiscal policy** which impacts upon spending in an economy by altering tax rates and levels of public spending. The following table highlights both the positive and negative impacts of a selection of political factors on an organisation.

Figure 2.1 Edinburgh trams.

Table 2.2 Impact of political factors

Political factor	Positive impact	Negative impact
Changing laws and legislation	The government could introduce environmental protection laws and policies such as 'Zero Waste Scotland' and, by complying, organisations will be seen in good light. This is good PR and can attract potential customers.	The government could increase the minimum wage so that organisations have higher wage costs. This will result in a lower profit for the year.
Changing income tax rates	The government could reduce taxes (money collected by the government to fund public spending), such as income tax. This will give customers a higher disposable income. This means customers will be more likely to spend money on a business' products, increasing sales.	The government could increase income tax. This will give customers a lower disposable income. This means customers would be less likely to spend money on a business' products, unless it is essential. This will reduce sales overall.
Changing VAT rates	The government could lower VAT (value added tax). This is a tax on goods and services. Reducing the VAT rate will make products more affordable for customers, increasing sales for a business.	The government could raise VAT (value added tax). This will increase the selling price which could put customers off purchasing products and reduce sales.
Changing corporation tax	Many types of businesses, such as limited companies, have to pay a tax on their profits (corporation tax). The government could lower the rate of corporation tax which would mean less money is taken from the business and given to the government, which would increase profits.	The government could raise the rate of corporation tax which means more money would be taken from the business and given to the government, which would reduce the profit of the organisation.
Public spending on infrastructure	The government could decide to fund the development of infrastructure. Examples include building new motorways, car parks, tram networks, and so on. This will increase the likelihood of attracting customers for businesses in these areas. Public spending also creates jobs, which gives people wages and enables them to spend money on other goods and services.	Public spending is a contentious issue as it only improves certain areas. For example, the new Edinburgh tram network will greatly improve Edinburgh's infrastructure, however, businesses in Glasgow will see no benefit. This is known as 'opportunity cost', i.e. the cost of spending money on one area is that it can't be spent in another.

Economic factors

Economic cycle

Economic factors arise from the state of the **economy**. An economy is
the state of a country or region in terms of the production and
consumption of products, and the supply of money. In other words,
when the UK economy is doing well, businesses produce more products,
which creates more jobs and leads to more people having more money
to spend. However, the economy alternates between good and bad times.
You will perhaps remember the global **recession** that hit in 2008, when
unemployment was high and businesses were going bust. This economic
activity is known as the **economic cycle** and is illustrated in Figure 2.2.

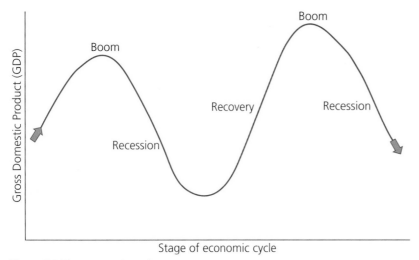

Figure 2.2 The economic cycle.

The economic cycle diagram illustrates the different stages of an
economy in terms of a country's **gross domestic product (GDP)**. GDP
is a figure that sums up the amount of goods and services produced and
consumed by a country, so GDP is a good indicator not only of output
and profits of businesses, but also of employment and the wealth of
citizens too. Table 2.3 describes each stage of the economic cycle and the
impact of each stage on businesses.

Table 2.3 Impact of the economic cycle stages

Stage	Definition	Impact
Boom	GDP and employment levels are very high.	Businesses can take advantage of the demand for products and the wealth of consumers by increasing prices. This will improve profits for the business.
	Demand for products is high.	However, a side effect is an increase in **inflation**. This is a rise in prices over time and often leads to wage rises, so people can afford to keep up with inflation.
Recession	GDP and employment levels fall.	Businesses have to react to a falling demand by making staff redundant, which will cost them redundancy payments and lose them the skills and knowledge of employees.
	Demand for products falls.	Prices will have to be cut to try and increase demand, which will lower the amount of profit a business can make and may even lead to losses.
Recovery	GDP and employment levels begin to rise.	Businesses can rely on consumers being in a better position to spend money due to rising employment, so therefore sales will increase.
	Demand for products increases.	Businesses can develop new products and start to increase prices, which will lead to bigger profits for the business.

Economic policy

It is the role of the government to try and control the economy through a number of measures, called economic policy. The **economic policy** of a government can be divided into two areas, fiscal policy and monetary policy.

1 **Fiscal policy** – A government's fiscal policy concerns the tax rates it sets and its level of public spending (as covered in the political section of external factors).

2 **Monetary policy** – A government's monetary policy is the ways in which it controls the supply of money into the economy and therefore affect spending. This can be done by varying **interest rates**.

Interest rates

Interest rates determine the percentage that is added to borrowings or savings. All financial institutions, such as banks or building societies set their own interest rates. However the government bank, the Bank of England, sets the **base rate** of interest. This is the minimum rate of interest that banks and building societies *must* apply to loans and savings.

By increasing interest rates the Bank of England attempts to curb spending and therefore reduce inflation.

By decreasing interest rates the Bank of England attempts to encourage spending in order to avoid a recession or to recover the economy. Table 2.4 highlights how this is achieved and the impact of interest rate changes on businesses.

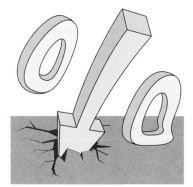

Figure 2.3 A drop in interest rates encourages consumer spending.

Table 2.4 The impact on business of changes in interest rates

Interest rate	Effect on savings	Effect on borrowing
Rise in interest rate	Customers are *more* likely to save due to attractive rates as they will earn more money on their savings. This means customers will spend less on businesses' products as they are saving their money instead.	Customers are *less* likely, or able, to take out loans or to spend using credit cards as they will have to pay back more money on their borrowing. This means customers will be able to spend less on businesses' products.
Reduction in interest rate	Customers are *less* likely to save as interest rates are unattractive, so are more likely to spend money on businesses' products.	Customers are *more* likely to borrow money as it is less expensive to pay back loans and credit card debts, so are more likely to spend money on businesses' products.

Exchange rates

An **exchange rate** determines the amount of one currency that can be bought using another currency. For example, if the exchange rate of £ pounds sterling to the € Euro is 1.25, it means for every £1 exchanged, €1.25 is given. The exchange rate of the £ pound sterling against foreign currencies changes on a daily basis.

A high value or 'strong' pound is caused by a high demand for the currency. If UK products are selling well abroad (known as **exports**) the pound will be in demand and the price will rise. The Bank of England can affect this too through interest rates, as high interest rates will attract savings from abroad and again the price of the pound will rise. Of course, the opposite is also true – a high demand for goods purchased from abroad (**imports**), low demand for exports and low interest rates will cause the demand for the pound to fall and therefore the price of the pound to fall too. Table 2.5 highlights the effect of exchange rate changes on businesses.

Table 2.5 The effects of exchange rate changes on businesses

Exchange rate	Effect on exports	Effect on imports
Strong pound	If the value of the pound is high compared to foreign currencies, UK exporters will struggle to sell their products abroad as they will be more expensive than foreign goods and sales will fall.	If the value of the pound is high compared to foreign currencies, imports will become cheaper. This will decrease costs for businesses that source materials from abroad which will increase their profits. It will also allow a lower selling price to be charged for products made in the UK to attract customers.
Weak pound	If the value of the pound is low compared to foreign currencies, UK exporters will be able to sell more goods to foreign countries as their goods will be less expensive for customers outside the UK.	If the value of the pound is low compared to foreign currencies, imports will become more expensive. This will increase costs for businesses that source their materials from abroad and may lead to an increase in prices.

WWW

The UK, and indeed the world, economy is always changing. It would be beneficial for your Higher Business Management studies for you to keep up to date with changes that are taking place and how these changes impact on organisations. You can keep informed at the following website: **www.economist.com**

Social factors

Social factors concern the ways in which *society* changes and the need for businesses to adapt in the same way. Social factors could be either a change in the **demographics**, the characteristics of the population, or a change in cultural behaviour. Table 2.6 highlights a selection of social factors and their possible impact on organisations.

Table 2.6 The effects of social factors on businesses

Social factor	Positive impact	Negative impact
UK's ageing population	This is a vast, and growing, market segment. Businesses that can produce products tailored for this market should succeed. Many potential customers in this segment are retired and well off so there is a potential to offer quality products at high prices.	Extensive market research must be carried out which costs time and money.
More women with professional careers	As more women are taking up high-profile professions and managerial roles they are waiting longer to have a family. As a result, couples are generally better off when they have their first child so businesses can offer high-quality maternity and baby products that sell for a high price.	More women will be taking maternity leave once they are established in their careers which will mean organisations have to consider flexible working arrangements, such as part time or job share. This will result in the organisation having to spend time recruiting and training replacement staff.

Evolving work–life balance	Less employees are working the traditional 9–5 working week. As a result, businesses must cater for the needs of a society that works around the clock for 7 days a week. This has led to a trend of convenience in the UK, e.g. 24-hour opening hours, e-commerce, etc. By meeting the convenience needs of customers businesses will ensure repeat custom.	Organisations have to provide more staff to work 24 hours a day, 7 days a week to meet customer needs, which will increase wage costs.
Changing fashion trends	Businesses can cater for the latest fashion trends and offer products that customers want, therefore increasing sales. An example of a current fashion trend that retailers ranging from Debenhams to Asda cater for is the 'onesie'.	Businesses have to spend time and money researching and developing new products. Some products also have a very short shelf-life.
Flexible working arrangements	Flexible working arrangements mean staff will be able to work at a time when they are most productive, which will improve quality in the organisation as well as raising morale. Additionally, businesses can save money on renting office space if more employees work from home.	Flexible working arrangements can lead to a lack of supervision and direction of staff, which can reduce productivity. Organisations may also have to provide staff with equipment such as smartphones and laptops so they can work at home, which can be costly.

Technological factors

Figure 2.4 Cloud computing is changing the way people work.

Technological factors concern the quickly evolving technological advancements that can impact on organisations, for example, faster broadband connections, cloud computing and social media. Table 2.7 highlights a selection of technological factors and the possible impact on organisations.

Hints & tips ⭐

Remember that technology can be an internal or an external factor. The main difference is that as an internal factor the concern is existing technology, which is the technology the business uses already, while as an external factor the concern is keeping up with technological developments, that is what technology the business needs to invest in to remain competitive. More specific uses of technology are covered throughout this book.

Table 2.7 The effects of technological factors on businesses

Technological factor	Positive impact	Negative impact
Cloud computing	Through technology such as Onedrive or Dropbox, organisations can save money on their own IT hardware. Additionally, they will not require as many IT staff to maintain equipment, saving on wage costs.	There is a heavy reliance on 'the cloud' performing. If internet connection is unavailable, the organisation won't be able to access files stored on the cloud, causing production to stop. There are also privacy and confidentiality issues regarding storing information on the cloud.

Social media	Having a social media (e.g. Facebook, Twitter) presence enables organisations to keep in touch with customers and raise their profile to a potentially world-wide market.	Social media can be used by customers to spread bad reviews about an organisation, leading to a poor reputation that could put customers off and cause them to take their business to the competition.
Wi-Fi	Organisations that provide a free Wi-Fi service are likely to attract customers who wish to use Wi-Fi for work or personal reasons, for example a customer choosing a Starbucks coffee house over an independent coffee shop because of Starbuck's free Wi-Fi.	There is a financial cost of setting up and maintaining Wi-Fi.
4G	4G will enable organisations' employees to communicate and download information while on the move much more quickly.	Not all areas are equipped with 4G capabilities, which could leave organisations in these areas behind.

Environmental factors

Environmental factors can either arise from the way in which the natural environment impacts on organisations or the ways that organisations act in an ethical and environmentally friendly manner. Table 2.8 highlights a selection of environmental factors and the possible impact on organisations.

Table 2.8 The effects of environmental factors on businesses

Environmental factor	Positive impact	Negative impact
Weather	A business could be impacted by spells of favourable weather, for example, during prolonged periods of snow the ski industry in Scotland will see an increase in customers.	Prolonged spells of adverse weather, such as snow, can affect the transport networks across the UK. This will make it difficult for deliveries of materials to arrive and for staff to get to work, therefore causing production to slow down or cease entirely.
Recycling	Organisations encourage recycling by their customers in order to impact less negatively on the environment. For example, retailers discourage the use of plastic bags and sell 'bags for life' which will lower the cost to the retailer of providing plastic bags and gain the company a favourable reputation for being 'environmentally friendly'.	Organisations need to undertake recycling, for example, of waste paper and printer cartridges, but it takes time, effort and money to recycle rather than just disposing of waste.
Carbon footprint	Organisations are encouraged to reduce their carbon footprint. This means to lower the amount of emissions from fossil fuels released into the atmosphere. Businesses that do this, for example by utilising renewable energy will eventually save money on fuel bills.	There is a financial cost associated with investing in renewable energy, for example, solar panels or wind turbines to power factories.

Competitive factors

Most businesses face **competition**. An organisation's competition refers to rival organisations that provide the same or a similar product and attempt to take their customers, attract new customers or keep their own customers. Many methods used by competition will be covered in the **marketing** chapter (see Chapter 6) but a select few examples are given in Table 2.9, including some positive ways that competition can impact on an organisation.

Table 2.9 The effects of competitive factors on businesses

Positive impacts	Negative impacts
Competition opening up a physical store right next to a business can be good as it provides more choice for customers and brings passing trade to the area.	The competition could lower prices, undercutting another business. Businesses will either have to lower prices too, reducing profits, or risk losing customers to the competition.
Competition improves a market as it brings with it more choice, new ideas and keeps prices low, which can benefit all businesses in the market.	The competition could launch new or improved products. Businesses will have to spend money researching and developing products to keep up with competition.

Competition policy

In 2014, the **Competition and Markets Authority** (CMA) was launched by the UK government. Its aim is to investigate markets and enforce **competition policy** in order to promote competition for the benefit of consumers.

Reasons for promoting competition

It is in the government's interest to promote competition for the following reasons:

- prices are kept low for consumers
- products and services are high quality
- customer service is good
- entire markets improve and grow, creating jobs and raising GDP
- healthy markets can attract foreign investment.

Impact of competition policy

Here are just some of the areas that competition policy covers and the impact it has on businesses:

- **Cartels** – Organisations cannot participate in **cartels**. This means colluding with other organisations to fix prices to make higher profits. If found guilty of participating in cartels, owners or management can be fined or even sentenced to prison.
- **Mergers** – The CMA can block mergers if it is likely to lead to a 'substantial lessening of competition' in any market.
- **Anti-competitive behaviour** – Organisations cannot use their dominant position in the market to charge drastically low prices, pay lower prices to suppliers or control the supply of goods to the detriment of the market.
- **Consumer protection** – Consumers have rights and are protected from unfair practices such as hidden charges and poor customer service.

  WWW

Read more about competition policy and the CMA: **www.gov.uk/ government/organisations/competition-and-markets-authority**

Activity 2.1

External factors, or PESTEC analysis, is a great way to *analyse* the threats and opportunities to an organisation that exist in the external environment.

1. Create a presentation using PowerPoint, Prezi, a mind-map, a poster or any other presentation method you like.
2. Decide on which market you wish to investigate, for example, soft drinks, health and beauty, sports, and so on.
3. After some initial research, choose which organisation you wish to investigate in more depth.
4. Using the internet, quality newspapers or your own knowledge, research and write about each PESTEC factor in relation to your chosen organisation.

Important! Don't just describe an example of the factor; make sure you explain how each one *impacts*, positively or negatively, on your organisation.

Key questions 2.2

1. Identify three different tax changes that can impact on organisations.
2. Compare fiscal and monetary policy.
3. Outline two social and two technological changes in recent years.
4. Describe one positive and one negative impact of competition on an organisation.

Essential question 2.2 ?

Explain the impact of two external factors on a large organisation.

Stakeholders

A **stakeholder** is an individual or group of people who have an interest in the success of an organisation. **Internal stakeholders** are from *within* the organisation, such as owners (or shareholders), managers and employees. **External stakeholders** are from *outside* the organisation, such as government, banks, customers, suppliers, pressure groups and the Inland Revenue (the government organisation responsible for collecting taxes).

Table 2.10 outlines the **interest** and **influence** of selected stakeholders.

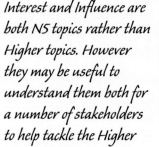

Hints & tips

Interest and Influence are both N5 topics rather than Higher topics. However they may be useful to understand them both for a number of stakeholders to help tackle the Higher level stakeholder topics.

Table 2.10 The interest and influences of selected stakeholders on businesses

Stakeholder	Interest	Influence
Owners	Profits in order to see a return on their investment.	Can invest more money. Can make important decisions.
Managers	May be given bonuses, pay rises or promotions based on the organisation's performance.	Can make decisions.
Employees	Want job security and perhaps a pay rise.	Can affect standard of work. Can take industrial action.
Customers	Demand a quality product/service and value for money.	Can take their custom elsewhere. Can spread good/bad word to others.
Suppliers	Want continued business and the business to pay its debts.	Can change prices. Can adjust the quality of supplies. Can change account terms.

Conflict of interest

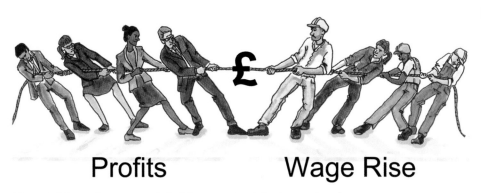

Profits   Wage Rise

Figure 2.5 Sometimes two stakeholder groups can't both get what they want.

Although all stakeholders want a business to succeed, they can often conflict in their individual aims. In other words, two stakeholders both cannot get what they want at the same time. Some examples of **conflict of interest** are given in Table 2.11:

Table 2.11 Examples of conflicts of interest

Conflicting stakeholders	Conflict example
Employees v. owners/managers	Employees want a pay rise, whereas owners want to maximise profits. *If employees get a pay rise it will lower the amount of profits the owner will receive.*
Customers v. owners/managers	Customers want low prices and value for money, whereas owners want to raise prices to maximise profits and meet their own objectives. *Low prices and high prices can't both happen! So businesses and customers 'meet in the middle', known as the* **equilibrium price**.
Suppliers v. owners/managers	Suppliers want to be paid as soon as possible ideally in cash, whereas the owners want trade credit to keep good cash flow in the business. *Suppliers and owners can also disagree on the prices of products, discounts, quality of supplies, delivery time and so on.*
Government v. owners/managers	Governments may want to introduce legislation to improve society, however owners may disagree with the legislation as it will impact negatively on their business. *For example, the Government raising the minimum wage will lower the profits of a business as wage costs will increase.*

Interdependence of stakeholders

Stakeholders need to work together if the business is to succeed. Some stakeholder groups rely on others to help them achieve their interests. This is known as the **interdependence of stakeholders**. Some examples of interdependence are given in Table 2.12:

Table 2.12 The interdependence of stakeholders

Interdependent stakeholders	Interdependent example
Owners/managers and governments	Owners/managers need governments to make good decisions, such as lowering taxes to improve the spending power of customers and therefore sales, while governments need owners to create jobs.
Owners/managers and suppliers	Managers need suppliers to provide quality raw materials and stocks to improve the quality of the finished product, while suppliers need managers to keep buying from them and keep them in business.
Owners/managers and customers	Owners need customers to buy their products and customers need a good quality of product and customer service from the owners of the business.
Owners and employees	Owners need employees to perform to their best to increase sales and profits through work rate or customer service, while employees need owners to make good decisions to keep the business profitable and their jobs safe.
Managers and employees	Employees and managers need to work together to help the business to succeed in order to keep their jobs secure.

Key questions 2.3

1 Describe the term 'stakeholder'.
2 Describe the interests the Inland Revenue has in an organisation.
3 Describe the influence of customers on an organisation.
4 Describe the interdependence of owners and governments.

Essential question 2.3

Describe two conflicts of interest that could exist between stakeholders.

Exam-style questions practice – Chapter 2

1 Describe ways in which a lack of finance can impact on an organisation. **(3 marks)**
2 Explain economic factors that can affect an organisation. **(5 marks)**
3 Explain the benefits to an organisation of having a strong corporate culture. **(5 marks)**
4 Describe the ways in which competition policy can affect an organisation. **(3 marks)**
5 Describe the benefits recent advancements in technology can have on an organisation. **(4 marks)**

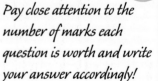

Hints & tips

Pay close attention to the number of marks each question is worth and write your answer accordingly!

Outcome 1.3: Decision-making

Decision-making

Types of decisions

Decision-making is essential in managing a business or organisation. The important thing to remember is that it is not just the managers at the top of the hierarchy that make decisions. There are however, three different types of decisions, strategic, tactical and operational, as illustrated in Table 3.1.

Table 3.1 Three types of decisions: strategic, tactical and operational

Type of decision	Length of decision	Decision maker	Purpose
Strategic	Long term	Senior managers	To meet the overall purpose and direction of the organisation, e.g. to grow the business.
Tactical	Medium term	Middle managers	To achieve the strategic decisions, e.g. launch new products to grow organically.
Operational	Short term, day to day	Supervisors/all staff	To react to situations as they arise, e.g. dealing with a customer complaint.

Mission statement

As part of the strategic decision-making process, organisations will release a mission statement, a written statement outlining the overall aims and objectives of the organisation.

A mission statement can allow a business to:
- let customers know of the overall aims and objectives of the business
- promote CSR aims
- attract quality staff, if they agree with the aims
- inform potential investors about the strategic goals of the business.

WWW

Ben & Jerry's have a very prominent mission statement based around three core values: product, economic and social. Take a look at their website and see for yourself.

www.benjerry.co.uk/values

SWOT analysis

An organisation can use a structured decision-making model known as a **SWOT analysis**. This allows them to look at their internal (*inside* the organisation) strengths and weaknesses, as well as external (*outside* the organisation) opportunities and threats. A SWOT analysis is often laid out in a grid (see Figure 3.1) for easy comparison of the organisation's position and to allow an informed decision to be made about future actions.

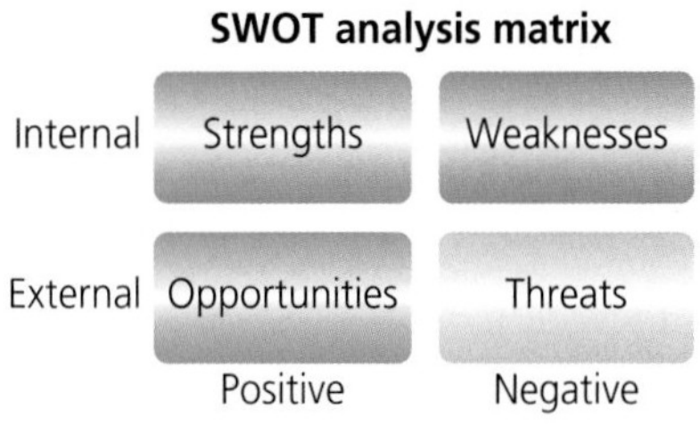

SWOT analysis matrix

	Strengths	Weaknesses
Internal	Strengths	Weaknesses
External	Opportunities	Threats
	Positive	Negative

Figure 3.1 SWOT analysis matrix.

Strengths

Strengths are things the organisation is good at. These could be:

- availability of finance
- well-known brands or products
- goods/services that make the most profits
- products that are 'benchmarks' in the market which competitors try to copy
- assets the business owns, such as a large modern factory, modern technology or a retail outlet in a prime location
- high quality staff and good staff morale.

Weaknesses

Weaknesses are things the organisation is ineffective at. These could be:

- lack of finance
- lack of technology
- poor customer service reputation
- faulty products
- products or branches that are making losses
- assets that are in a state of disrepair, such as a crumbling factory or ageing fleet
- untrained staff or low staff morale.

Opportunities

Opportunities are the possible chances a business could take that arise due to something happening outside the organisation's control. These might be:

- a competitor going bust, so the business could take on its customers
- a boom period in the economy that the business could exploit
- customer tastes and fashions falling in line with an organisation's specialism
- governments introducing favourable legislation
- advancements in technology that the business could exploit, for example, e-commerce.

Threats

Threats are things that might impact on a business achieving its aims or making positive decisions. These may be:

- competitors' actions, such as cheaper prices or better-quality products

- a downturn in the economy, such as a recession
- customer tastes and fashions changing, away from those the business specialises in
- governments introducing legislation that impacts badly on the organisation
- advancements in technology that could leave the business behind its rivals.

Table 3.2 Advantages and disadvantages of using SWOT analysis

Advantages of using SWOT	Disadvantages of using SWOT
Identifies strengths and allows a business to build upon them.	A SWOT analysis is very time consuming, which can slow down decision-making.
Identifies weaknesses and allows them to be addressed.	A SWOT analysis is a very structured process which can stifle creativity and gut reactions from managers.
Identifies opportunities and allows them to be exploited.	A SWOT analysis can generate many ideas however, it doesn't help pick the correct one.
Identifies threats and allows them to be turned into opportunities, e.g. embracing advancing technology not allowing it to leave the business behind.	A SWOT analysis produces a result that reflects the opinions of those who carry it out which could lead to bias.
Time is taken to analyse the business' current position so no rash decisions are made.	A SWOT analysis considers information that is available at a particular moment and may become outdated quickly.

Activity 3.1

On your own or in pairs, carry out your own SWOT analysis on an organisation of your choice.

1 Copy the SWOT diagram in Figure 3.2; you can do this either on paper or using a table in Microsoft Word.
2 Using the internet, newspapers or your own knowledge, find out information for each section and complete your diagram.

Factors affecting the quality of decisions

Organisations often face a variety of issues when making decisions. There are many internal factors that can affect the quality of decision-making.

Human resources

The human resources, people within the organisation, can affect decision-making in the following ways:
- managers' ability, training and experience to make good decisions
- how much risk the managers will take when making decisions
- staff resistance to change
- managers' ability to handle stressful and complex situations
- the likelihood of overpowering managing directors or owners overturning decisions made by middle management.

Availability of finance

Whether or not the organisation has or can get hold of finance can impact on decision-making in the following ways:
- whether finance is available to exploit the opportunities, address weaknesses or build on strengths

- financial constraints may mean an organisation cannot choose the best solution to a problem.

Technology

The availability of technology to help make informed decisions can affect the quality of decisions, for example:

- **Spreadsheets** can improve the accuracy of calculations using formula and perform 'What if?' statements to calculate the projected outcome of a decision.
- **Databases** can improve the speed of decision-making by making it easy to search for information quickly using queries and sort functions.
- **Email** can be used to communicate information regarding decisions to many employees at once and attachments containing information can be sent which reduces printing costs.
- **Internet** sites can be used to find out a vast amount of information to make an informed decision.
- **Video-conferencing** (also known as tele-conferencing or simply video-calling) can reduce the need for managers to travel to meetings, saving time and travel costs.

Figure 3.2 A management meeting using video-conferencing.

Other factors

- Company policy may restrict the decisions made or the options that are available to decision makers.
- Lack of opportunity to consult others may mean that decisions are poor and staff resist change.
- Time constraints can restrict the time taken to decide on a course of action or to implement a final decision.
- The quality of the information available on which to base the decision may be poor. In other words it could be out of date, biased, not relevant or incomplete, for example.

Role of a manager

The roles of a manager have developed over the years. The main roles are based on the work of business management theorist, Henri Fayol. He outlined the five functions of management.

- **Plan** – The function of management is to be looking ahead, seeing potential opportunities, or problems, setting targets and strategies. The importance of planning can be remembered by the phrase: 'If you fail to plan, you plan to fail!'
- **Organise** – Management must set tasks for other employees that need to be carried out to achieve set targets.
- **Command** – Managers should issue instructions to employees.
- **Co-ordinate** – Management must bring together the resources of the business to achieve the overall objectives that have been set.
- **Control** – Managers need to ensure they are measuring and correcting the activities of the organisation. A manager looks at what is being done and checks this against what was expected.

Modern-day roles

Since Henri Fayol outlined the five functions of management, managers have adopted more modern roles. Nowadays, in addition to the five functions that Fayol identified, managers must:

- **Delegate** – give subordinates the authority to carry out management-level tasks. This helps lessen the manager's workload and achieve the next role.
- **Motivate** – give his team a reason to enjoy their work. Workers are motivated in different ways (see Chapter 4).

Remember

... the role of a manager with the mnemonic POCCC-DM.

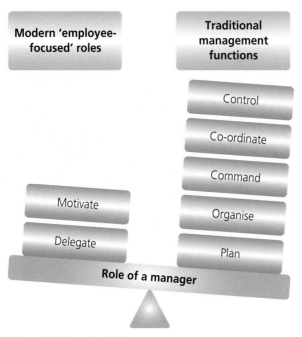

Figure 3.3 The role of the manager.

Hints & tips

Be prepared to answer questions in context, e.g. the role of a manager in decision-making or the role of a finance manager, as well as the general roles/functions of a manager as described here.

Assessing the effectiveness of a decision

Managers will assess the effectiveness of a decision in the following ways:

- Measuring sales levels to see if they have increased
- Analysing profit levels to see if they have improved
- Interview staff to assess their opinion of the decision
- Monitor staff morale, absence and turnover following major decisions
- Finding out from customers about improvements in service
- Track changes in share prices to major decisions

Exam-style questions practice – Chapter 3

1. Distinguish between strategic and operational decisions. (**3 marks**)
2. Discuss the use of a structured decision-making model, such as SWOT analysis. (**5 marks**)
3. Describe the role of a manager in an organisation. (**5 marks**)
4. Describe factors that affect quality decisions being made. (**4 marks**)
5. Explain the advantages of using technology to aid decision-making. (**4 marks**)

Chapter 4

Outcome 2.1: Management of People

What you should know

There are four main parts to this outcome. By the end of this outcome you should be able to:

1 **Describe** approaches that could be used to manage human resources effectively.
2 **Describe** approaches that could be used to motivate staff to improve effectiveness.
3 **Explain** how employee relations can impact on the success of a large organisation.
4 **Describe** the impact of current employment legislation.

Management of human resources

The management of people in an organisation is the job of the human resources department. Its role is to:

- ensure the organisation has the personnel it needs
- train staff
- motivate staff
- ensure positive employee relations
- comply with current employment legislation.

Workforce planning

The number of personnel in a workforce is constantly changing. Organisations often have to recruit new employees or remove existing employees to meet the needs of the businesses effectively.

Reasons for workforce changes

New staff may be needed for the following reasons:

- to meet increasing demand for existing products
- to develop new products to satisfy demand

- to assist in opening new stores/factories
- to help enter new markets
- to respond to flexible working arrangements.

Existing staff may be removed or leave for the following reasons:
- to respond to falling sales/demand for products
- to take up positions with competitors or other local employers
- because employees retire, take sick leave, go on maternity leave, and so on.
- the business needs different employees with new skills.

Steps in workforce planning

Workforce planning is about deciding how many and what types of workers are required and when. There are several steps involved in workforce planning:

1 The organisation analyses the potential demand for its goods/services and decides how many staff are needed and what skills are required to meet this demand. The organisation will take PESTEC factors into account (see Chapter 2).

2 The organisation analyses the profile of its current workforce to determine the need for new staff and the skills that need to be developed in existing staff.

3 The organisation 'closes the gaps' to ensure that it has the workforce required to provide the goods/services to meet their objectives by:
   a) recruiting and selecting new staff
   b) training existing staff
   c) retaining existing staff through motivation methods.

Recruitment and selection

Recruitment is the process of generating potential employees to apply for a particular job in an organisation.

Internal or external recruitment?

An organisation can recruit for staff from either within the organisation (internal) or from outside the organisation (external).

Table 4.1 gives examples of where an organisation may advertise for each.

Table 4.1 Examples of job advertising methods

Internal	External
Staff noticeboard	Job centre
Organisation's intranet	Newspaper adverts
Internal email to all or selected staff	Websites such as Monster or S1 Jobs
Company newsletter	Recruitment agencies – specialist organisations that are experts in recruiting and selecting the best staff for other organisations. This is an example of outsourcing (see Chapter 1).

Internal recruitment

Table 4.2 Advantages and disadvantages of internal recruitment

Advantages	Disadvantages
The vacancy can be filled quickly.	Applicants are drawn from a very limited pool so the organisation may not hire the *best* person for the job.
The employee knows the organisation which saves induction training costs and time.	Promoting one employee will consequentially create a vacancy in their old post.
The employee is known to the organisation and can be trusted to do a good job.	The organisation misses out on a chance to bring in fresh, new ideas and new skills to the organisation.
The organisation saves money on external advertisement costs.	Employees can resent a fellow colleague being promoted over them. This can cause conflict and relations to become strained.
Employees will be more motivated as they know there is a chance of promotion.	

External recruitment

Table 4.3 Advantages and disadvantages of external recruitment

Advantages	Disadvantages
Fresh, new ideas and skills are brought into the organisation.	Candidates do not know the organisation so induction training will have to be carried out, taking up production time and costing money.
There is a wider pool of candidates to choose from.	Such a potentially vast pool of candidates can mean it takes longer to choose suitable applicants for interview.
It avoids creating a further vacancy in the organisation.	The organisation does not know the successful candidate, which carries a risk that they may not be suited for the job, or worse are untrustworthy.
It avoids the jealousy and resistance that is often created by one employee being promoted over others.	Existing staff may be de-motivated as they perceive that there is no chance of internal promotion.

Selection methods

Selection is the process of choosing the correct person from the pool of applicants that have applied for the job.

1 **Application forms and CVs**. An application form is a document, produced by the employer, containing questions that applicants answer to provide details of their skills, experience and qualities. This is often more useful than a **curriculum vitae (CV)**, which is usually a two page document listing a person's work experience, qualifications and personal experiences. By using an application form, every applicant answers the same questions, making it easier to compare their answers with those of another applicant than with a CV.

2 **Interviews**. All interviews are designed to compare the applicant's responses to questions against a set criteria. Interviews can take various forms: with one manager (**one-to-one**), with a single manager, one manager after another (**successive**) or in front of a number of people at the same time (**panel**).

Table 4.4 Advantages and disadvantages of interviews

Advantages	Disadvantages
Interviews find out how an applicant reacts under pressure.	Some applicants can train specifically for interviews and say what the interviewers want to hear but may not be the best person for the job.
Interviews give an indication of the applicant's personality and character.	Interviews can be highly stressful. This means an organisation may miss out on quality employees who underperform in the pressure of an interview.

3 **Testing**. Tests provide additional information about an applicant; however, they can be time consuming to carry out and may put applicants under too much pressure to perform as they would once they get the job.

Table 4.5 contains possible tests an organisation can carry out.

Table 4.5 Tests used during selection

Attainment test	This allows an applicant to demonstrate their skills, e.g. ICT skills by completing a typing test.
Aptitude test	This assesses if a candidate has the natural abilities and personal skills for the job, e.g. a prospective customer services assistant roleplaying a scenario with an angry customer.
Psychometric test	This assesses an applicant's personality and mental suitability for a job. There are no right or wrong answers, instead the test gives an insight into how an applicant thinks and if they would fit into the organisation.
Intelligence/IQ test	This measures a candidate's mental ability; used for jobs where candidates may be solving problems.
Medical test	This measures physical fitness levels which may be required for certain jobs, e.g. the fire service, armed forces, etc.

4 **Assessment centres**. Organisations use assessment centres to see a large number of applicants at the same time. Applicants take part in a variety of team-building and role-play exercises as well as a number of tests. This allows an organisation to scrutinise applicants, to assess their suitability for the job, as well as how they interact with others.

Table 4.6 Advantages and disadvantages of assessment centres

Advantages	Disadvantages
Allows an organisation to really scrutinise applicants over a longer period of time.	A venue will need to be hired, if an organisation doesn't have its own assessment centre, which is expensive.
Assesses how applicants interact with others.	Several managers will need to be sent to the centre to conduct and supervise the tests, losing production time.
Assesses how applicants react to role-play scenarios that mimic real work situations.	Such tests require careful planning and preparation, all of which takes time.
Reduces the chance of interviewer bias as the results are a true reflection of each applicant's abilities and not just what one manager thinks.	

5 **References**. This is using references, or information from referees. These are used to confirm that the candidate is who they say they are, and that they are reliable. References are usually requested from previous employers and/or someone else with authority, such as the head teacher at the candidate's school.

6 **Trial periods**. This involves an applicant being employed for a short period of time, a day, a week or longer, before they are offered the position permanently, to make sure they are capable of doing the job, and that they are reliable and trustworthy. This avoids an organisation making a mistake by offering a job to someone who isn't suitable, and potentially having to go through lengthy **discipline** and **dismissal** procedures.

Training

Training means to improve the skills or knowledge of staff within an organisation. Table 4.7 lists the general advantages and disadvantages of training.

Table 4.7 The general advantages and disadvantages of training

Advantages	Disadvantages
It helps to improve the quality of products/service as employees have better skills.	It can be costly to an organisation if outside training centres or trainers are used.
It's motivational for staff as it makes them more confident to do their job and they feel the business is interested in developing them.	It can lead to lost production time.
It can be used to develop skills to cope with change in an organisation, such as the introduction of new technology.	Staff may leave after being trained.
It reduces the number of workplace accidents since staff are more aware of procedures.	
A good training programme can attract high-quality staff.	

Induction training

This is training for *new* staff. Often staff are given an introduction to the organisation and a tour of the workplace where they can meet colleagues and are given any important health and safety requirements. Staff are also given basic instructions on the tasks they will need to carry out.

Table 4.8 Advantages and disadvantages of induction training

Advantages	Disadvantages
Staff become familiar with the organisation quickly and feel settled.	Prevents staff from starting their work immediately.
Important health and safety instructions are covered.	Existing staff are needed to carry out induction training, losing production time from them as well as the new employees.

Off-the-job training

This is training away from the workplace, either at a training centre or college.

Table 4.9 Advantages and disadvantages of off-the-job training

Advantages	Disadvantages
Staff can concentrate fully on learning about the job without any distractions.	It can cost a lot of money to send staff to training centres.
Current staff are not distracted/hindered by new employees training around them.	Nothing is actually contributed by those being trained to the organisation while training is taking place.

On-the-job training

This is training while the employee is actually carrying out the job, such as a newly qualified teacher who actually teaches classes while training.

Table 4.10 Advantages and disadvantages of on-the-job training

Advantages	Disadvantages
The employee actually contributes to the organisation while they are training.	Mistakes can be made.
Some employees learn better by doing the work rather than reading/hearing about it.	Coaching the new employee can slow the coach (experienced employee) down while they are coaching them through tasks or demonstrating tasks to them.

On the job training can take the form of:
- **Coaching:** An experienced employee taking a trainee through a task.
- **Demonstration:** Being shown the task by a designated trainer.
- **Job rotation:** Sampling different roles to experience what is involved.
- **Work shadowing:** Spending time with someone doing their day-to-day job so a trainee can see first-hand how it is done.

Staff development

The human resources department must ensure that staff continue to develop their skills and knowledge. Not only will this motivate staff, as they will feel the organisation is taking an interest in developing them, but staff will also be more able to adapt to changing external factors. Staff can be sent on training courses, take part in training days at work or use one of the following methods of development:

Training schemes

Organisations can offer staff the chance to take part in **training schemes**. These are intense programmes of training that will equip staff with enhanced skills so they are either in a good position for a pay rise or for a promotion, for example, through a management training scheme.

Case study 4.1
Vue

Vue cinemas have a **management-training scheme** in place that allows employees to work their way up through the various levels in the management structure. Vue cinemas have a centralised structure, with the head office in London, while each division is grouped by location, with cinemas all over the UK, for example, in Glasgow, Edinburgh, Stirling and Aberdeen. A typical employee starts off working as a customer assistant at a local cinema and, if they show promise, can be placed on a management-training scheme. Employees on the scheme attend training courses and have to prove they have met the learning objectives of each course at their **appraisals** with their line manager. Once their manager has agreed that they have met the objectives, they can be promoted to a team leader position and eventually, to a manager or even a general manager position.

Discussion points

In pairs, groups or on your own, consider:

1 Why would a training scheme such as Vue's motivate staff?
2 Do you know of any other organisations that provide management training schemes? If not, take some time to use the internet to find some.

Table 4.11 Advantages and disadvantages of management training schemes

Advantages	Disadvantages
The organisation benefits from highly skilled staff.	Work time can be lost throughout the training.
Staff are motivated, which lowers staff turnover.	The organisation will have to pay staff more after training is complete.

Work-based training and qualifications

Organisations can also offer staff the chance to gain formal qualifications while working. In Scotland many of the qualifications are based on the SVQ (Scottish Vocational Qualifications) framework. SVQs are work-related qualifications that reflect the skills and knowledge required to do a specific job. This qualification can be achieved through an **apprenticeship** scheme. This is common in manual trades, such as joinery or plumbing, and they are mostly delivered in the workplace with some days spent at a local college when required.

Professional qualifications such as accounting or engineering examinations can also be studied for through work-based training.

Table 4.12 Advantages and disadvantages of work-based training

Advantages	Disadvantages
Employees gain a recognised qualification and learn through practical application of their learning.	Staff may leave for a better job after gaining their qualification.
Employees can contribute to the organisation while training.	Organisations usually pay for the training and examinations.

Virtual learning

A virtual learning environment is a way to access learning and teaching tools, to help staff gain knowledge and training, through the internet. These are similar to the various 'e-learning' platforms you may have used in your school or college, such as Glow or Edmodo. Using a virtual learning environment, staff can access learning and assessment materials, submit assignments and even interact with other students and trainers via webcam. Staff can use virtual learning for any form of training, such as induction training, work-based qualifications or training schemes.

Table 4.13 Advantages and disadvantages of training using a virtual learning environment

Advantages	Disadvantages
Trainees can access materials from home or while travelling, and at any time of day.	Some trainees will be more reassured by face-to-face contact.
Trainees can interact with trainers through video-conferencing or chat facilities.	The virtual learning environment can be costly to set up.
Saves money on sending trainees to courses and on printing training materials.	There's no guarantee that staff will complete all the training in the virtual learning environment.

Key questions 4.1

1 Distinguish between recruitment and selection.
2 Describe two reasons for workforce planning.
3 Describe three steps involved in workforce planning.
4 Describe the use of trial periods as a selection method.
5 Describe two ways to develop staff.

Essential question 4.1 **(?)**

Describe two approaches that could be used to manage human resources effectively.

Motivation

It is in any organisation's best interest to have motivated staff. The advantages of having motivated staff include less absenteeism, better performance, lower staff turnover and better employee relations.

Motivation theories

You read in Chapter 3 about management theorist Henri Fayol's work, describing the role that managers have in organisations. We will now explore the theories of three more management theorists to gain an understanding of what motivates employees.

Maslow's hierarchy of needs

In 1943, Abraham **Maslow** said that humans had five sets of needs (motivators), which come in a particular order. As each level of needs is satisfied, the desire (motivation) to fulfil the next set kicks in. Everyone starts with the lowest, most basic need and works up until the highest need is reached. A person will not be motivated by the higher needs until their basic needs are met. Maslow's hierarchy is best illustrated as a pyramid (see Figure 4.1).

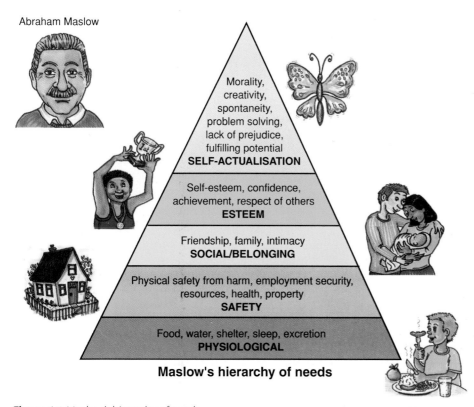

Abraham Maslow

Morality, creativity, spontaneity, problem solving, lack of prejudice, fulfilling potential
SELF-ACTUALISATION

Self-esteem, confidence, achievement, respect of others
ESTEEM

Friendship, family, intimacy
SOCIAL/BELONGING

Physical safety from harm, employment security, resources, health, property
SAFETY

Food, water, shelter, sleep, excretion
PHYSIOLOGICAL

Maslow's hierarchy of needs

Figure 4.1 Maslow's hierarchy of needs.

Table 4.14 Implications of Maslow's hierarchy of needs for motivating staff

Need	Description	Implications for motivating staff
5 Self-actualisation	To realise potential and have status in life. Maslow wrote: 'What a man can be, he must be.'	Opportunities for creativity and personal growth, promotion opportunities.
4 Self-esteem	To feel worthy and respected.	A job title that stands out from others, recognition of ones achievements in front of peers.
3 Love and belonging	To fulfil social needs such as friendship and family.	A good team atmosphere, open plan offices, friendly supervision.
2 Safety and security	To feel safe at work, at home, financially and physically.	Safe working conditions, job security, fair wage rises in line with inflation.
1 Physiological needs	The basic needs for bodily functioning and staying alive; fulfilled by eating, drinking and going to the toilet.	A living wage, basic safe working environment, access to toilet facilities and running water.

McGregor's Theory X and Theory Y

In 1960, Douglas **McGregor**, an academic at the Massachusetts Institute of Technology, wrote about two different motivational theories. McGregor believed that there were two distinct perceptions or assumptions that managers have of what motivates their employees. He called these perceptions **Theory X** and **Theory Y**.

Table 4.15 Impact of Theory X and Theory Y management perspectives on motivating staff

Manager's perspective	Description	Impact on motivating staff
Theory X	Employees dislike work and try to avoid it at all costs. Employees have no ambition and prefer to avoid responsibility, delegation or empowerment. Employees only work to earn wages to satisfy their needs and wants.	Employees need to be closely supervised and controlled. A tall management structure is required with a narrow span of control. Managers need to command, coerce and even threaten employees to carry out tasks.
Theory Y	Employees are satisfied with their job and are self-motivated to meet personal goals and organisational objectives. Employees seek responsibility and are happy to accept it. Employees work to fulfil their own personal goals for status and recognition.	A culture of trust can be created in the organisation which can be developed through flatter structures, delegation and empowerment. Employees are motivated by the self-actualisation needs at the top of Maslow's hierarchy so respond well to promotion and status. Employees respond well to development such as management training schemes.

Hertzberg's motivator–hygiene theory

In 1959, Frederick **Hertzberg** wrote the motivator–hygiene theory (also known as the two-factor theory) of motivation. According to Hertzberg, employees are motivated by two sets of factors: motivator factors and hygiene factors.

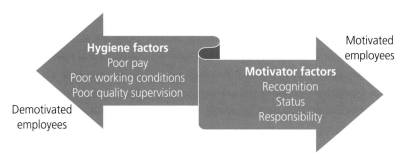

Figure 4.2 Hertzberg's theory of motivation.

Hygiene factors

Hygiene factors will not motivate employees, but if they are not met, they can *lower* motivation. These factors could be anything from clean toilets and comfortable chairs, to a reasonable level of pay, job security, and supervision, procedures and policies that employees are happy with.

Motivator factors

Motivator factors will not necessarily lower motivation if they are absent or not used, but can be responsible for *increasing* motivation. These factors are also linked to the needs at the top of Maslow's hierarchy and could involve rewarding employees with status and recognition, potential for promotion and delegated responsibility.

Methods of motivation

So, now you know why employees need to be motivated and, through the different theories presented here, the different needs of employees that an employer is required to meet. Management can use the different management theories to attempt to motivate staff through a number of measures.

Basic motivation methods

Table 4.16 Basic motivation methods

Motivation method	How it motivates employees
Fair pay	Employees work to earn money to satisfy their needs and wants. If they don't think they are receiving a fair amount of pay for their work they will be de-motivated and their productivity will decrease.
Payment methods	Organisations can use a number of payment methods to motivate staff: **Commission** – Salespeople can be offered commission, which is a percentage of the sales they make, motivating them to sell more. **PRP** – Performance-related pay, sometimes called a 'bonus', this is an extra payment on top of the basic wage for meeting agreed targets. **Piece rate** – When the employee is paid per item they produce, which encourages a high work rate, however, the quality of work may drop. **Overtime** – When an employee works longer than their contractual hours, normally at a higher rate of pay, this encourages extra production to meet demand. **Share–save schemes** – Employees save regular amounts which can be turned into shares in the business to be kept or sold at a profit. Employers can add to the shares or even give some to staff for free in order to motivate them.
Incentives	Non-financial incentives could be offered, e.g. holidays, cars, discounts and private healthcare.
Permanent contracts	Employees need to feel that they have job security. Organisations should avoid the use of temporary contracts where possible. Permanent contracts will make employees feel more secure and they will get on with their jobs.
Good working conditions	Employees need to feel that their working conditions are safe. As Hertzberg states, good working conditions won't necessarily motivate employees but bad working conditions will demotivate them. However, an improvement in working conditions, such as better equipment, a new office or company car may motivate staff for a short while.

Advanced motivation methods

Some employees will need more than a contract, pay and good conditions to be motivated at work. Organisations need to find ways to satisfy the 'Theory Y' employee, according to McGregor. This can be achieved through providing Hertzberg's 'motivator' factors and meeting Maslow's top two hierarchy needs too!

Table 4.17 Advanced motivation methods

Motivation method	How it motivates employees
Staff appraisals	Regular meetings with a manager are known as appraisals. These motivate employees as they are told what they are doing well and given targets to aim for. They can also be targeted for promotion.
Recognition	Employees who want to progress in their career respond well to recognition, such as an 'employee of the month scheme'.
Development opportunities	Employees will want to develop their skills, for example through a management training scheme, so they are able to be identified for promotion opportunities and improve their status in the organisation.
Empowerment	Empowerment means giving staff the authority to make their own decisions. Managers can delegate part of their responsibility to an employee and let them decide how best to carry it out. This will give employees a sense of job satisfaction.

Employee participation	Organisations can utilise a variety of methods to involve employees in decision-making:
	Worker-director – When a worker-director position is created, a low-level employee such as a factory worker or a sales assistant is given a seat on the Board of Directors. Worker-directors have no voting rights; however they present their views and the views of fellow workers to the board. Ultimately, employees feel that they have a say in decision-making.
	Works councils – also known as consultative committees, are groups made up of an equal number of employees and managers. The group discusses major suggestions for change in the organisation and have joint decision-making powers. This reduces resistance to change from employees.
	Quality circles – (see page 126) involve employees being consulted on how to improve the standard of the products they produce. This makes employees feel involved in decision-making and that they can make a difference.

Case study 4.1

Starbucks

The CEO of Starbucks, Howard Schultz, considers that the reason for Starbucks' success is not coffee but employees. The managers in Starbucks treat each employee equally and all of the staff are called 'partners', even the supervisors. In order to narrow the gap between managers and employees, managers also co-work with the lowest level of staff in the front line. Due to this, they can maintain good relations and create a much closer and friendlier atmosphere than other workplaces. Not only do employees enjoy their jobs but customers are also affected by their enthusiasm. Such an enthusiastic and vibrant atmosphere is key to the culture of Starbucks. It's even in their mission statement, to 'inspire the human spirit', and employees can be recognised for capturing the spirit in their work by being given the 'Spirit of Starbucks Award'. Starbucks managers have regular, informal appraisals with each employee, which can just be a quick chat, to ask them how they are doing and if they (the manager/organisation) can meet the employee's needs or even just to ask if they need a day off! Employees can also be sent on college courses to gain qualifications.

Employees are also asked to participate in quality circles and to let management know if they have a good idea, from a quick operational solution to a major strategic change. All employees are offered a great deal of incentives, for instance, discounts on Starbucks' products and medical insurance. They also have their own share–save scheme, called 'Bean Stock' to allocate stock dividends to all employees. Because of this, all managers and employees have the same goal; they are motivated to increase sales to earn more profit.

Discussion points

In pairs, groups or on your own:

1 Identify five methods Starbucks use to motivate employees.
2 Consider which motivation method would motivate you or your group the most and why?
3 Consider which of Starbucks motivation methods exist to motivate the Theory X employee?
4 Consider which of Starbucks motivation methods exist to motivate the Theory Y employee?

Leadership styles

Employees respond well to different managers. This is because all managers have a different style of leadership. These styles are described in Table 4.18 below.

Table 4.18 Advantages and disadvantages of the different leadership styles

Leadership style	Advantages	Disadvantages
Autocratic: Authority and control is retained by the leader. Managers tell employees what to do.	There are clear expectations of what needs to be done. Decisions can be made quickly. This works well when the manager is the most skilled or knowledgeable in the team.	There's no opportunity for delegation or empowerment, de-motivating some staff. There's a lack of creativity in decision-making as it is retained with senior management.
Democratic: Communication and employee participation are key. Managers let employees have a say in decision-making.	Employees feel motivated as they have a say in decision-making. The manager has the final say but employees can contribute, which can encourage creativity and help solve complex problems.	Mistakes can be made if workers are not skilled or experienced enough to participate in decision-making. Some employees can be less productive than they would be under an autocratic manager.
Laissez-faire: A rough translation of the French phrase 'laissez-faire' is 'let them be'. Managers with this style do exactly that, they don't issue instructions or supervise staff, they just let staff carry out their jobs.	Employees are highly empowered to make decisions and only seek manager's assistance when they need help, which motivates employees. This can create a very relaxed work environment.	Lack of direction can lead to objectives not being met. This can only work in highly professional environments where workers are self-motivated, such as technology companies or creative industries.

Factors affecting leadership style

- **The task**: A complex task, such as deciding on new company policy, will require more direction from management (autocratic); a creative task, such as designing new packaging, would benefit from a hands-off approach (laissez-faire).
- **Time available**: There may be little time to complete a project which means less time for discussion on how to achieve it, so a more autocratic style will be required.
- **Skills of staff**: Highly skilled and competent staff will need less supervision and direction, so a democratic approach will work.
- **Motivation of staff**: Highly motivated employees such as 'Theory Y' employees can be trusted to have the self-discipline to make their own decisions and complete tasks without instruction and supervision.

- **Leader's own personality**: Leaders may lack personable qualities and automatically lead in an autocratic style. Similarly they may be too friendly and nice to be autocratic!
- **Group size**: Democratic styles can lead to confusion if the number of staff in a group is too large. Large groups benefit from the clear direction of autocratic leadership.
- **Corporate culture**: The culture in an organisation can persuade managers to use specific styles, for example, an open and relaxed environment found in technology firms lends itself to a laissez-faire approach.
- **Availability of finance**: Democratic and laissez-faire styles can delegate spending to departments and individuals. A lack of finance may lead to autocratic styles being adopted in order to control spending.

Key questions 4.2

1 Outline three benefits of motivating staff.
2 Describe two methods of payment that will motivate staff.
3 Compare the perceptions of a 'Theory X' employee with a 'Theory Y' employee, according to McGregor.
4 Describe the impact on motivating staff of any three stages of Maslow's hierarchy of needs.
5 Describe Hertzberg's motivator–hygiene theory.
6 Describe the three leadership styles a manager could adopt.

Essential question 4.2

Describe two approaches that could be used to motivate staff to improve effectiveness.

Employee relations

Employee relations refers to the relationships that exist between management and employees in an organisation.

Methods to promote positive employee relations

Appraisals

An **appraisal** is a two-way meeting between an employee and another member of staff to discuss the employee's performance and to set targets for the future. An appraisal is traditionally a formal meeting between an employee and their line manager; however, modern methods include peer appraisal, 360-degree appraisal and informal appraisal.

Table 4.19 Advantages and disadvantages of appraisals

Advantages	Disadvantages
Positive feedback can be given which motivates the employee.	Negative feedback can be given which demotivates employees.
Targets will be set for the employee which motivates them and gives them a goal to work towards.	An employee might be set unrealistic targets which puts them under pressure.
Training needs can be identified which can motivate staff and increase quality standards.	Too many development needs may be identified which will stress the employee.
Pay rises and bonuses can be awarded after a successful appraisal which will motivate staff and ensure their work rate improves further.	Some employees resent the appraisal system. They feel under pressure and as if they are being checked up on.
Employees can be identified for promotion, which will increase their loyalty to the organisation.	Appraisals are time consuming to carry out which will result in lost work time during the time they are being conducted.
Strong relationships are formed between managers and employees as they are given the opportunity to have a professional discussion.	

Informal appraisal

An informal appraisal takes place whenever the line manager feels it is necessary. This is just a quick chat, while working or during a coffee break, perhaps highlighting something an employee is doing well or to give advice on how to improve.

Table 4.20 Advantages and disadvantages of informal appraisals

Advantages	Disadvantages
Feedback is current to the employee's tasks and actions, so it's more likely to affect change than waiting until a formal review.	Informal appraisals can become *too* informal and advice can fail to be taken on board.
Employees are more relaxed than in a formal appraisal so are more receptive to advice.	No record of feedback or targets is kept.

Peer appraisal

A peer appraisal is when the review interview is carried out by a colleague at the same level in the organisation as the employee.

Table 4.21 Advantages and disadvantages of peer appraisals

Advantages	Disadvantages
Employees may relax more and react better to a review given by a colleague.	Personal relationships between peers could result in the appraisal being ineffective.
Relationships with line managers are not harmed through judgements or weaknesses being highlighted.	Bias could wrongly highlight an employee for a pay rise or promotion.

360-degree appraisal

The most complete method is the 360-degree appraisal. In this scenario, whoever conducts the appraisal, such as an HR manager, peer or line manager, interviews fellow employees, supervisors and subordinates about the performance of the employee.

Figure 4.3 A 360-degree appraisal offers performance feedback from many different people.

Table 4.22 Advantages and disadvantages of 360-degree appraisals

Advantages	Disadvantages
A complete profile of the employee is gained.	Some employees may find it difficult to be critical of their colleagues.
Areas of subjectivity, such as character and leadership skills are measured.	Time constraints can limit the quality of responses from so many people in the organisation.

Contemporary working practices

Modern working practices have evolved due to the following factors:

- More women are taking up managerial and professional roles so organisations need to be flexible to work around family commitments.
- There has been a dramatic increase in tertiary and quaternary employment (see Chapter 1) which do not require the same 9–5 hours, in a set place of work, in the same way as factory work in the secondary sector requires.
- There has been an increase in self-employment due to government training schemes and incentives for entrepreneurs.

Figure 4.4 Flexible 'third' spaces are becoming more common to move employees away from the office and the distractions of home.

As a result of these changes, employers have had to introduce a range of **flexible working practices** which are described in Table 4.23.

Table 4.23 Positive and negative impacts of new working practices

Working practice	Positive impact	Negative impact
Flexitime: Employees choose their own hours as long as they work their contracted number of hours per day/week/month.	Employees can't be disciplined for poor timekeeping as long as they work their contracted number of hours. Employees can work around family commitments, such as school drop off and pickup times.	It's difficult to arrange formal meetings unless 'core time' is set when employees must be in the office. However, this limits meetings to core time which can be difficult to arrange.
Homeworking: Employees work from home but keep in touch via the use of ICT, such as email. Employees can visit the office for meetings or to use hot desks, for example, to print a report.	Employees can save on travel time which means they can get more work done. Organisations can reduce office space if employees work from home, therefore cutting costs.	It is difficult for managers to supervise the work and monitor its quality. Employees that work this way still feel under pressure to be 'seen' to be working so may, for example, send unnecessary emails to their team or line manager, which actually decreases productivity. Relationships with colleagues and managers can break down if employees are often away from the office.
Third spaces: Spaces such as coffee shops or parks are adopted by businesses to encourage workers to relax and socialise with others while working.	Employees work where and when suits them best which can improve the quality of their work. Informal interactions with others can encourage creativity and positive employee relations.	Some employees prefer the structure of an office environment and the advice they can receive from their line manager. Formal meetings can be hard to arrange, especially at short notice.

Motivated staff

For employee relations to be positive in an organisation, firstly staff need to be motivated. A variety of methods of motivating staff, as detailed earlier in this chapter, should be used to ensure all staff are motivated to work hard.

Employee participation

Secondly, employees need to feel that they have a say in what happens in the organisation. This could be through **employee participation**, such as works councils or worker directors, as covered earlier in this chapter.

Consultation

Employees respond well if they are consulted on any major changes that are about to take place, especially if it will impact on their working day, such as the implementation of new procedures. If staff are not consulted, it will lead to poor employee relations and resistance to change.

Case study 4.2
BMW

When BMW announced the launch of the new MINI they knew it would mean a major change to the procedures at their Oxford factory. They wanted to take the chance to improve employee relations and not let the change harm relationships and communication. Firstly, BMW consulted staff about the changes taking place in the factory. Employees from the factory floor made it clear that they wanted to work as a team *with* management on the new MINI project. So, secondly, BMW hired extremely experienced and talented managers to work on the project, which helped employees feel confident that those in authority knew what they were doing and were qualified to lead the team. Thirdly, each manager adopted a democratic leadership style, allowing all employees to have an input in decision-making. This employee participation helped foster a culture of teamwork at BMW. The results spoke for themselves too; absenteeism fell dramatically and the rate of production increased by 40 per cent.

Discussion points

In pairs, groups or on your own:

1   Consider what other methods of employee participation could BMW have used?
2   Consider why do you think absenteeism dropped at BMW?
3   List all the methods BMW used to improve relations with employees. Why you think they worked?

Negotiation

Employees and management often need to come to an agreement on very serious changes, such as changes to pay and working conditions. In this situation, employees benefit from using **collective bargaining**. This means to speak as a group and not as a number of individuals, which gives employees a stronger voice when negotiating. For large employee groups, this can be done through a **trade union**.

External institutions

Often, employees need assistance from external institutions in order to come to agreements with their employers, especially if disputes occur.

Trades unions

A trade union is an organisation that represents a group of employees. Members benefit from the collective bargaining power of the trade union, the experience of the union leaders who represent them and the legal powers the union has should matters need to be taken to court. Examples of trades unions are shown in figures 4.5 and 4.6.

Figure 4.5 UNISON – union for public sector workers other than teachers, such as NHS employees.

Take a look at the website of the largest union in the UK
www.unitetheunion.org and consider the tasks below. You can discuss the points or type up your findings.

1 Find out about all the different industries the union represents.
2 Find out about what different employees are fighting for.

ACAS

When a trade union cannot come to an agreement with an employer on behalf of its members, the organisation can involve ACAS. This is a government-funded organisation which attempts to solve disputes in the workplace to stop them going to court. ACAS stands for the Advisory, Conciliation and Arbitration Service.

Figure 4.6 Unite the union – the largest union in the UK, covering all industries such as finance, automotive and IT.

- **Advisory**: ACAS are experts on all HR matters, such as legislation. ACAS can provide advice to organisations to help them understand HR policy and avoid disputes going further. ACAS also offers training to organisations. ACAS's belief is that 'prevention is better than cure'.
- **Conciliation**: A conciliator is similar to a referee. Conciliation involves an impartial ACAS conciliator discussing the dispute with both parties to help them reach a better understanding of each other's position and to reach an agreement before going to arbitration or court.
- **Arbitration**: An arbitrator (in this case ACAS) makes a final decision on a dispute, based on the evidence presented by both parties. Arbitration is voluntary, so both sides must agree to go to arbitration; they should also agree that they will stand by the arbitrator's decision. Arbitration by ACAS avoids matters going to court, which can be costly, take up many hours of work time and be stressful for both parties.

Find out more about ACAS for yourself at the following website:
www.acas.org.uk

CBI

The Confederation of British Industry (CBI) is a large and powerful business group that represents many employers. While employees have trades unions to go to for assistance, employers have the CBI looking out for them. The CBI represents all major industries and can use its size and voice to campaign (known as 'lobbying') for government influence that will benefit their members, such as campaigning for more investment in 'green' infrastructure or subsidising broadband developments.

WWW

Take a look at the different campaigns the CBI currently has running:
www.cbi.org.uk/campaigns

Grievances

Grievances are concerns, problems or complaints raised by an employee. Examples could include working conditions, disputes between staff and changes being introduced.

The employee should raise these concerns with their manager. If a worker has a grievance against their manager, they should contact their HR Department, their trade union or ACAS.

In order to keep employee relations positive, it is best to solve grievances early to stop them escalating into formal disputes. Managers should be trained to deal with grievances and should encourage employees to be open and honest about their feelings. They should not blame or judge employees, should try to understand concerns and need to assess if a simple solution can be made. For example, an employee might simply have been paid the wrong amount which can be easily fixed by looking at their contract and contacting the payroll department.

Discipline

Organisations should have **company policies** (rules) regarding employee conduct and set procedures in place to deal with employees who fail to follow them. These rules could cover: poor attendance, conduct and personal use of telephones and the internet.

The following would be an appropriate **disciplinary procedure**, should any of the above rules be breached.

1 Deal with cases of minor misconduct or unsatisfactory performance, or an employee's first breach of company policy informally. A quiet word is often all that is required to improve an employee's conduct or performance.
2 Employers should deal with issues promptly, fairly and consistently.
3 Where some form of formal action is needed, investigations should be carried out to gather and establish all the facts of the case.
4 Employees should be given the facts of the case and allowed to put their response forward.
5 Employees have the right to be accompanied to any formal disciplinary meeting (for example, by a trade union representative) and be allowed to appeal against any formal decision made on sanctions to be issued. Sanctions could include:
    - a formal written warning
    - a final written warning, if it is a serious or repeat offence
    - suspension of employment, with or without pay
    - demotion
    - dismissal.

For minor offences, employees could escalate through these sanctions until the sanctions are exhausted; however, serious offences, such as theft from the organisation, could lead to immediate dismissal.

Remember

An organisation dealing with grievances, discipline and dismissal in the correct manner is key to ensuring positive employee relations.

Dismissal

A dismissal is when an employer terminates the employee's contract. Dismissal should be the last resort in terms of sanctions for breaking company policy and should only be used after formal disciplinary procedures have taken place.

- Employers must be able to give account of the policies the employee has broken and the procedures and sanctions that have been used before dismissal.
- Employers should use a fair and consistent procedure when dismissing employees.
- Employees have a right not to be unfairly dismissed. Employers could contact ACAS for advice on what constitutes unfair dismissal, for example, dismissing a female employee for absence during pregnancy.

Activity 4.2

A fun activity to revise the *Management of People* topic is to produce an 'induction booklet' for an organisation of your choice. You could:

- use your own work place, if you have a part-time job
- choose somewhere you *want* to work in the future! Most large business websites will have plenty of information on their HR department
- complete this activity using the work place of a friend or family member, if you can't find out the information you need online.

Create the booklet in Microsoft Word, or on paper if you prefer, and include:

1 an introduction to the company and the recruitment/selection process
2 why it is great to work there. (This is where an employer shows off their positive employee relations, how they motivate staff and their 'corporate culture' to new staff!)
3 why training is important
4 methods of training:
   a) description of each method
   b) what each method includes (use real examples)
   c) the benefits – to the staff *and* to the organisation
   d) the costs to the business (to highlight how nice they are being)
5 grievance and discipline procedures.

Impact of positive employee relations

- Employees will have their chance to discuss changes or grievances so will feel happier and more secure in the workplace.
- Disputes are less likely to arise as the workers will have been consulted and understand why changes are necessary.
- The workforce will be committed to the organisation and will help ensure it meets its objectives.
- It will be easier to introduce change within the organisation as staff will be more flexible with suggestions from management.

- The organisation will gain a good image for treating its employees correctly and maintaining good employee relations. Customers, investors and potential employees might be attracted to the organisation.

Impact of negative employee relations

If employee relations are poor, an organisation can experience:
- poorer employee performance due to low morale
- increased staff turnover as employees leave for a better work environment
- increased staff absenteeism
- less co-operation of staff during periods of change
- an increase in grievances and discipline problems
- industrial action in extreme cases.

Industrial action

Industrial action occurs when employee relations are poor and employees and employers cannot agree how to resolve issues or problems in the organisation. Table 4.24 contains methods of industrial action that *employees* can take and the impact each has on the organisation.

Table 4.24 Types of industrial action taken by employees and their impacts on the organisation

Method	Description	Impact
Go slow	Employees work at a slower rate than normal.	Production rates will slow down and costs of production will rise *if* employees are paid hourly.
Work to rule	Employees only complete the tasks specified in their contract or job description.	Employees refuse to do anything extra such as quality circles or development tasks so the business will be less responsive to change.
Sit in	Employees remain in the workplace but do not work.	Production will stop and management cannot bring in replacements.
Overtime ban	Employees refuse to do any overtime (hours over those specified in their contracts).	The organisation won't be able to fulfil any rush orders or cope with increased demand.
Strike	Employees refuse to work; this is the last resort.	No products will be produced or services given to customers. Customers will go to the competition and may not return.
Picketing	Employees demonstrate outside the workplace to make their concerns known to the public.	This can result in bad publicity for the organisation which can put customers or potential employees off. Bad publicity can also result in the company's share price falling.

The *employer* can also take industrial action against the employees if they are unhappy with them.

Table 4.25 Types of industrial action taken by employer and their impacts on the employee

Method	Description	Impact
Overtime withdrawal	Management refuses to give employees extra hours.	Employees lose the chance to earn extra wages; however, on the other hand, the organisation will not be able to cope with any increase in demand.
Lock out	Management locks employees out of a factory or workplace.	Employees do not get the chance to work and earn money; however, production stops completely.
Close	A factory or branch is closed completely.	Staff are made redundant or have to relocate; however, drastic action like this can result in both market share and share price falling.

Key questions 4.3

1. Describe three methods of appraising an employee.
2. Describe the role of the following external institutions:
   a) ACAS
   b) CBI
   c) Trades unions.
3. Outline two factors an organisation should consider when disciplining an employee.
4. Describe the term 'grievance'.

Essential question 4.3

Explain two ways employee relations can impact on the success of a large organisation.

Employment legislation

Legislation is the laws that are introduced by the government. It is the role of the human resources department to take account of employment legislation and ensure it is followed accurately and consistently within an organisation. Failure to follow legislation can result in poor employee relations and grievances being raised by employees.

Equality Act 2010

❑ **Replaces previous anti-discrimination laws** (e.g. Sex Discrimination Act) with a single act to make the law simpler and to remove inconsistencies.

❑ **The act covers nine protected characteristics** that cannot be used as a reason to treat people unfairly. Every person has one or more of the protected characteristics, so the act protects *everyone* against unfair treatment.
These are:
  ☞ Age, disability, gender, race, marriage status, pregnancy and maternity, religion or belief, sexual orientation and gender reassignment.

❑ **There are seven different types of discrimination** under the new legislation.
These are:
  ☞ Harassment – this is behaviour that is deemed offensive by the recipient due to a protected characteristic.

  ☞ Victimisation – this occurs when someone is treated badly because they have made or supported a grievance.

  ☞ Direct discrimination – where someone is treated less favourably than another person because of a protected characteristic, e.g. a job advertised as 'not for males'.

  ☞ Indirect discrimination – when a rule or policy applies to everyone but disadvantages a person with a protected characteristic, e.g. a promotion being for over 30s.

  ☞ Associative discrimination – discrimination against someone because they are associated with another person who possesses a protected characteristic.

  ☞ Discrimination by perception – thinking someone has a characteristic and discriminating against them.

  ☞ Harassment by a third party – employers are liable for the harassment of their staff or customers by people they don't themselves employ, e.g. when outsourcing part of the business.

Figure 4.7 Equality Act 2010.

National Minimum Wage Act 1998

❑ This act makes it illegal to pay an employee below a certain amount per hour.
❑ Employees must meet the age criteria to qualify for each minimum rate and can take action if they are not paid the correct rate.
❑ Employers must calculate work-related costs, such as renting tools or cleaning uniforms, and ensure employees are paid above the minimum wage *after* these costs are deducted.
❑ This act may conflict with the Equality Act and see a rise in the employment of young workers to reduce wage costs.
❑ Any increase to the minimum wage by the government will increase the costs to the business and lower profits, for example the government raised the rates in October 2015 to:

Age of employee	Rate
21 and over	£6.70 per hour
18 to 20	£5.30 per hour
16 to 18	£3.87 per hour
Apprentices*	£3.30 per hour

Apprentices 19 or over and in their 2nd year or more are entitled to minimum wage.
NB – from April 2016, the Government will introduce a new mandatory National Living Wage (NLW) for workers aged 25 and over, initially set at £7.20.

Figure 4.8 National Minimum Wage Act 1998.

Employment Rights Act 1996

❑ An employee must be given a written *contract of employment* particulars within two months of starting, this contract will state:
  ☞ Rate of pay, hours, holiday entitlement, etc.
  ☞ Type of contract, e.g.
   • Permanent: employment lasts until either party gives the required notice of termination.
   • Temporary: is usually for a set period of time to fill a vacancy, such as a maternity leave.
   • Fixed term: a fixed and definite period that the contract will run for, e.g. a seasonal contract, such as a summer job.
❑ Employees have a right to:
  ☞ an *itemised pay slip*
  ☞ *maternity and paternity leave*
  ☞ *flexible working*
  ☞ *redundancy payments if they are made redundant.*

Figure 4.9 Employment Rights Act 1996.

Health and Safety at Work Act 1974

❑ It is the duty of every *employer* to ensure the health, safety and welfare at work of all employees, for example:

☞ The provision and maintenance of machinery and equipment so they are safe and without risks to health.

☞ The provision of training and instruction on safety issues, particularly regarding dangerous chemicals and equipment.

☞ Employers should prepare a written statement of their general health and safety policy and ensure employees are aware of it, including any updates.

❑ Employees' duties include regarding care of their own and other employees' health and safety, such as reporting of incidences or accidents, for example.

Offices, Shops and Railway Premises Act 1963

❑ This is the original health and safety legislation that sets out more specific laws regarding safety at work, such as cleanliness, overcrowding, temperature, ventilation, lighting, toilet facilities, supply of drinking water, for example.

Figure 4.10 Health and Safety legislation.

 WWW

Take a look at government legislation in more detail for yourself at the official legislation website:

www.legislation.gov.uk

Key questions 4.4

1 Identify three characteristics protected under the Equality Act 2010.
2 Outline three types of discrimination according to the Equality Act 2010.
3 Describe three types of contract that can be offered to an employee.

Essential questions 4.4

1 **Identify** a current employment legislation act.
2 **Describe** two effects of the law identified in question 1 on employees or the organisation.

Use of technology in managing people

Here is a summary of how technology can be used in the human resources function.

● The internet can be used to advertise vacancies online, increasing the number of potential applicants.

● Video-conferencing can be used to interview applicants. This saves time and travel costs but allows body language and facial expressions to be analysed, as well as the applicant's general appearance to be seen, unlike telephone interviews.

- Email can be used to organise training or appraisals, allowing many employees to be contacted at once.
- E-diaries can be used, allowing meetings and appointments to be scheduled more easily. Subordinates can also see their superiors' e-diary, and vice versa, so that meetings can be arranged without clashes occurring.
- Virtual learning platforms can be used for training purposes.
- ICT, such as laptops and email, can allow employees to work away from the office.

Exam-style questions practice – Chapter 4

1 Explain the impact of industrial action on an organisation. **(4 marks)**

2 a) Describe factors that would affect the leadership style of a manager. **(5 marks)**

   b) Distinguish between the following leadership styles: autocratic and laissez-faire. **(2 marks)**

3 Explain methods of employee participation that an organisation could use. **(2 marks)**

4 Discuss the use of flexible working methods. **(6 marks)**

5 Explain the impact of negative employee relations on an organisation. **(4 marks)**

6 Discuss the advantages and disadvantages of external recruitment. **(6 marks)**

7 Describe the main features of the Employment Rights Act 1996. **(4 marks)**

Chapter 5

Outcome 2.2: Management of Finance

What you should know

There are three main parts to this outcome. By the end of this outcome you should be able to:

1 **Describe** sources of finance suitable for large organisations.
2 **Describe** the purpose of financial statements.
3 **Describe** the use of ratios.

Hints & tips

The finance chapter has always given many Higher Business Management students the fear, but don't think this! Make sure you revise finance because, although it is actually a very small section compared to others, it must still come up in the exam!

Managing finance

The finance department ensures the business has the money it needs to operate effectively by working out its financial position. It does this by:

- monitoring cash flow, by producing **cash budgets**
- monitor performance, by producing **financial statements**
- controlling costs, by identifying increases in costs and enforcing cut backs
- providing information for decision-making, through **ratio analysis**.

The role of a manager in the finance department can also be summed up using the seven roles of a manager (as detailed on pages 46–47). The finance manager's role is to prepare budgets (plan), arrange finance to be in place (organise), and so on.

Sources of finance

A business can be financed via a number of different sources and there are advantages and disadvantages to each source as shown in Table 5.1.

Table 5.1 Advantages and disadvantages of different sources of finance

Source of finance	Internal/ External	Short term/ Long term	Advantages	Disadvantages
Owner's personal finance: Includes personal savings and money borrowed from family and friends.	Internal	Short	This allows the owner to keep control of the business. It can reduce the amount to be borrowed from other sources.	It can be difficult to withdraw savings once they are invested in the business. There is a risk that the owner could lose his savings if the business fails.
Retained profits: A business holding back profits from previous years.	Internal	Short	This can be used to make larger purchases, such as assets or for bulk buying.	A business can find it more difficult to grow if it regularly uses retained profits, especially to solve short-term cash-flow problems.

Sale of assets: Selling something that the business no longer needs.	Internal	Short	Money can be raised from the sale of an asset to boost cash flow. The money does not need to be repaid.	If the finance is required urgently, the business may have to sell the asset for less than it is worth.
Sell and lease back: Selling an asset and leasing it back.	Internal	Short	Money can be raised from the sale of an asset to boost cash flow. The business passes over responsibility for maintaining and renewing equipment to the leasing company.	Leasing over a long period of time can be expensive – ultimately, the business may pay back more than it received from the sale.
Share issue: Selling shares in the business. PLCs sell on the stock market. Ltds sell shares privately.	External	Long	Very large sums of money can be raised through the sale of shares. The money does not need to be repaid.	Dividends have to be paid to shareholders. It can be expensive to advertise and organise the sale of shares.
Debentures: Loans borrowed from individuals through the stock market.	External	Long	Control of the business is retained. These can be paid back over a long time.	Interest must be paid annually, even if a loss is made, unlike with shares where dividends are only paid out if profits are made.
Bank overdraft: A facility which allows a business to spend more money than is in its bank account.	External	Short	This is usually easy for a business to arrange with its bank. It allows a business to continue to pay business expenses, despite there being no money in its bank account.	High interest rates are usually applied by the bank for borrowing money in this way. The overdraft can be withdrawn by the bank at any time and must then be repaid.
Trade credit: Allows a business to buy goods from suppliers and pay for them at a later date.	External	Short	This allows a business to sell stock at a higher price and earn a profit before the bill needs to be paid. It helps a business to keep going when cash flow is poor.	Discount for prompt payment is lost. Suppliers will be reluctant to continue to offer credit if a business does not pay within the agreed credit period.
Debt factoring: A business sells its unpaid customer invoices to a factoring company. The factoring company then collects and keeps the customers' debts.	External	Short	Responsibility for collecting the debt is passed on to the factor, saving the company time and effort. Cash flow is improved by receiving an advanced payment of the debts from the factor.	The business has to sell the customer debt for a reduced amount, i.e. it receives less money than is actually owed. Factoring companies are usually only interested in large amounts of debt.

Grants: Money is given to a business from central or local government, the EU or the Prince's Trust.	External	Long	These are often offered as an incentive and a way of helping a business get started or expand. The money does not need to be repaid.	They can be complicated to apply for and can require the business to meet certain requirements. Grants are usually one-off payments that are not repeated.
Bank loan: A bank agrees to lend a business money for a specific purpose, for a fixed period of time. Regular repayment instalments are put in place.	External	Long	The business can budget for the repayments. Purchases of essential equipment can be made in advance and paid back over a number of years.	Interest has to be repaid along with the loan amount. Small businesses may find it more difficult to secure a loan and often need to pay higher interest rates, as they are a greater risk.
Leasing: Renting vehicles or equipment.	External	Long	The business does not need to spend large amounts of money to purchase the vehicles/equipment it needs. The leasing company is responsible for maintaining and renewing the equipment.	The business does not own the asset/s it is renting. Rental costs can build up over a long period of time – it may be cheaper in the long run for the business to buy the equipment.
Hire purchase: A business can buy an asset by paying an initial deposit and then monthly payments for a fixed period of time.	External	Long	Expensive equipment can be bought with only an initial deposit. The asset, e.g. a delivery van, is owned by the business at the end of the repayment period.	The business does not own the asset until the last instalment is paid. It can be an expensive form of borrowing if interest rates are high.
Mortgage: A large sum of money borrowed from a bank or building society secured on a property.	External	Long	It can be paid back over a long period of time, e.g. 25 years. The interest rate charged is often lower than the rate on a bank loan.	Interest has to be repaid along with the loan amount. The mortgage provider owns the property until the last repayment is made. This means the business could lose the property if it does not keep up the repayments.
Venture capitalists: Organisations that invest in established businesses in return for equity (ownership percentage).	External	Long	Large amounts of investment can be gained by established businesses. Venture capitalists are willing to take on more risky investments than banks.	Venture capitalists have an equity stake, which means control and a share of profits are given up.
Business angels: Individuals who invest in start-up businesses in return for equity.	External	Long	Business advice is often provided as well as finance. Business angels are willing to take a risk on new businesses.	Business angels have an equity stake, which means control and a share of profits are given up. This is only suitable for smaller amounts of investment for new businesses.

Factors affecting sources of finance

The source of finance chosen by or available to a business will depend on a number of factors:

Table 5.2 Factors affecting sources of finance

Factor	Description
Short-term finance required	An organisation may only need finance for a short term, perhaps to cover a cash flow problem, so an overdraft could be used.
Long-term finance required	An organisation may need long-term finance, perhaps to fund the purchase of property, so would choose a mortgage.
Interest rates	An organisation will choose the finance with the lowest interest rate available.
Payback term	The quicker the payback term, the less interest the organisation will pay on borrowing.
Size and type of organisation	Organisations are restricted to certain sources of finance, for example, a public sector organisation cannot sell shares and has to rely on government funding.

Key questions 5.1

1 Outline one internal and one external source of finance.
2 Describe three factors affecting the source of finance.
3 Compare venture capitalists with business angels.
4 Describe one advantage and one disadvantage of debt factoring.

Essential questions 5.1

1 **Describe** two sources of finance for a large organisation.
2 **Justify** your suggestions in essential question 1 above.

Financial statements

Users of financial statements

Table 5.3 Users and purposes of financial statements

User	Purpose
Owners	To assess profits and to inform decision-making.
Employees	To ensure their jobs are secure.
Inland Revenue (HMRC)	To ensure the business is paying the correct amount of tax.
Trades unions	To assess if their members are due a pay rise.
Competitors	To measure their success against each other.
Investors	To assess the potential for investment.
Lenders	To decide whether or not to give a loan.

Income statement

An **income statement** (trading, profit and loss account) calculates the profit made from buying and selling, known as **gross profit** and the profit made after expenses are deducted from gross profit, known as **profit for the year**.

Table 5.4 defines the terms that appear in an income statement:

Table 5.4 Terms that appear in an income statement

Term	Definition
Sales revenue	The amount of money made from selling goods or services.
Cost of sales	The amount of money spent on selling goods. Calculated by: (opening inventory + purchases) – closing inventory
Gross profit	The profit made from buying and selling. Calculated by: Sales revenue – cost of sales
Expenses	Running costs incurred throughout the year.
Profit for the year	The profit made after expenses are deducted from gross profit. Calculated by: gross profit – expenses

Example 5.1

Income statement for Example PLC for year ended 31 Dec 2014	£000	£000
Sales revenue		1000
Less Cost of sales		
Opening inventory (Stock)	50	
Add Purchases	250	
	300	
Less Closing inventory (Stock)	25	
Cost of sales		275
Gross Profit		725
Less Expenses		
Wages	250	
Administration	100	
Advertising	75	425
Profit for the year		300

Hints & tips ★

Note the use of the words Less (−) and Add (+) in the income statement to indicate how the different totals are calculated.

Case study 5.1

Aikman, Boag & Craig – ABC Ltd

You have been given the following financial statement for Aikman, Boag & Craig, ABC Ltd. Study the information and complete the Discussion points below.

Income statement for ABC Ltd for years 2011 to 2013			
	2011	2012	2013
	£000	£000	£000
Sales revenue	5000	6000	8000
Less Cost of sales	2000	2100	2500
Gross profit	3000	3900	5500
Less Expenses	1500	1300	1600
Profit for the year	1500	2600	3900

Hints & tips

You don't need to be able to prepare these financial statements; however, you do need to be able to interpret them. Understanding how the statements are calculated will help you do this.

Discussion points

In pairs, groups or on your own:

1 Describe the trends in the following:
   a) profits
   b) expenses
   c) sales revenue.
2 Suggest possible reasons for the trends you described above.

Statement of financial position

The **statement of financial position** (balance sheet) shows the items a business owns, known as **assets**, the items they owe, known as **liabilities**, and the overall **value** of the business. Table 5.5 defines the terms that appear in a statement of financial position:

Table 5.5 Terms that appear in a statement of financial position

Term	Definition
Non-current assets (Fixed assets)	Items owned for a period of more than one year.
Current assets	Items owned for a period of less than one year.
Current liabilities	Items owed for a period of less than one year.
Working equity	The ability to pay short-term debts. Calculated by: current assets – current liabilities
Net assets employed	This is the value of non-current assets added to the working equity figure (if positive – if working equity is negative it will be subtracted from non-current assets).
Non-current liabilities	Long term debts of the business, e.g. bank loan, debentures etc.
Net assets	The overall value or worth of the business. Calculated by: net assets employed – non-current liabilities.
Equity	This shows how the business has been financed, e.g. the capital, retained profits, etc. It should add up to the exact value of total net assets.

Example 5.2

Statement of financial position for Example PLC as at 31 Dec 2014			
	£000	£000	£000
Non-current assets (Fixed assets)			
Premises			1500
Vehicles			175
Equipment			100
			1775
Add **Current assets**			
Closing inventory (Stock)	25		
Cash	700	725	
Less **Current liabilities**			
Bank overdraft	150		
Trade payables (Creditors)	50	200	
Working equity			525
Net assets employed			2300
Non-current liabilities			
Bank loan			500
Net assets			1800
Equity			
Share capital		1500	
Profit for the year		300	**1800**

Case study 5.2

Debbie's Deli

You have been given the following financial statement from Debbie's Deli. Study the information and attempt the Discussion points below.

Statement of financial position for Debbie's Deli PLC as at 31 Dec 2014			
	£000	£000	£000
Non-current assets (fixed assets)			
Premises			800
Vehicles			200
Fixtures & fittings			100
			1100
Add **Current assets**			
Closing inventory (Stock)	50		
Cash	400	450	

$\Rightarrow$

⇨

Less **Current liabilities**			
Bank overdraft	250		
Trade payables (Creditors)	150	400	
Working equity			50
Net assets			1150
Financed by:			
Share capital		?	
Profit for the year (Net profit)		150	1150

Discussion points

In pairs, groups or on your own:

1 Suggest reasons for such a low working equity figure.
2 Describe the effect a low working equity figure has on total net assets.
3 State the missing share capital figure.

Cash budgeting

Cash-flow problems

Cash budgets need to be prepared to help organisations remain **liquid**. Liquidity refers to the cash-flow situation in an organisation. Organisations need to remain liquid in order to have the funds to pay off their debts.

In addition to arranging **sources of finance**, if an organisation encounters cash-flow problems from the following sources, there are various ways to solve them:

Table 5.6 Solutions to cash flow problems

Source	Solution
Too much money tied up in stock	Use just-in-time (JIT) stock control (see page 117).
	Sell off excess stock, e.g. through a 'sale'.
Too many credit sales	Offer cash discounts to encourage customers to pay in cash.
Too long a payment period for credit sales	Charge higher interest on credit sales to encourage customers to pay sooner.
Not enough credit purchases	Switch suppliers to those with interest-free credit available on purchases.
High amounts of spending on non-current assets	Pay for non-current assets in instalments, such as paying for a vehicle using hire purchase.
Increasing expense costs	Look for ways to reduce expenses, e.g. spend less on rent by selling online through e-commerce.
Too many drawings by owners	Charge higher interest on drawings to discourage owners from withdrawing money from the business.
Not enough sales revenue	Adapt the marketing mix (see page 93) to encourage more sales, e.g. lower prices.
Too many unpaid debts	Sell debts to debt factoring companies.

A cash budget is a financial statement used for the following reasons:
- to predict a positive cash-flow situation (**surplus**)
- to predict a negative cash-flow situation (**deficit**)
- to allow investment to be planned during a surplus
- to allow action to be taken to avoid a deficit
- to be compared with actual figures and used to measure the performances of individual departments or divisions.

Table 5.7 defines the terms that appear in a cash budget:

Table 5.7 Terms that appear in a cash budget

Term	Definition
Opening balance	The amount of cash available at the start of the month.
Total receipts	The total cash received during the month.
Cash available	The amount of cash available to spend. Calculated by: opening balance + total receipts
Total payments	The total amount of cash spent during the month.
Closing balance	The amount of cash available at the end of the month. Calculated by: cash available – total payments

Example 5.3

Cash budget for Example PLC for 3 months Aug–Oct 2014						
	£	£	£	£	£	£
	Aug		Sep		Oct	
Opening balance		1000		3800		450
Receipts						
Cash sales revenue	5000		4000		2800	
Loan	1000		–		–	
Total receipts		6000		4000		2800
Cash available		7000		7800		3250
Payments						
Purchases	1800		1900		2000	
Wages	800		800		800	
Rent	600		600		650	
Purchase of van	0		4000		0	
Loan interest	0		50		100	
Total payments		3200		7350		3550
Closing balance		3800		450		−300

Hints & tips

Notice the opening balance is the closing balance from the previous month!

The following interpretations can be made by analysing the information in the cash budget for Example PLC.

Table 5.8 Interpreting the cash budget of Example PLC

Problem	Interpretation	Solution
Cash sales are falling.	This could be caused by seasonal factors such as the business selling goods suitable for summer months only. There may also be other external factors at play, such as a recession or rising interest rates.	The business should engage in marketing activities, for example, lowering prices or launching promotions, such as advertising or buy-one-get-one-free (BOGOF) deals to encourage custom.
Purchases are increasing.	The business is tying too much money up in stock. The stock is not selling, yet they have ordered more and more.	Use just-in-time (JIT) stock control.
Expenses are increasing.	The business is paying increasing costs for expenses, for example rising rent costs in October.	Switch to cheaper premises or sell online to cut rent costs dramatically.
Negative closing balance.	The business had a deficit in October which means their payments outweigh their receipts. This leaves the business unable to pay off other debts and expenses.	Arrange more finance in the short term, such as another loan, overdraft or attract investment, for example, through business angels.

Case study 5.3
Clemod PLC

You have been given the following financial statement from Clemod PLC. Study the information and attempt the Discussion points below.

Cash Budget for Clemod PLC for 3 months Nov–Jan 2014–15						
	£	£	£	£	£	£
	Nov		Dec		Jan	
Opening balance		500		750		?
Receipts						
Cash sales revenue	3000		4500		2000	
Loan	0		0		1000	
Total receipts		3000		4500		3000
Cash available		3500		5250		3580
Payments						
Purchases	1400		1,800		1,800	
Wages	800		800		800	
Rent	550		570		590	
Computer purchase	0		1,500		0	
Loan interest	0		0		100	
Total payments		2750		4670		3290
Closing balance		750		580		290

⇨
Discussion points

In pairs, groups or on your own:

1 Identify the opening balance for January.
2 Outline four sources of cash-flow problems faced by Clemod PLC.
3 Suggest solutions to the problems you have identified in the previous question.
4 Explain possible reasons for the increase in sales in December.

Key questions 5.2

1 Outline the use three different users of financial information may have for the information.
2 Suggest two reasons competitors are interested in the financial statements of an organisation.
3 Outline three features of an income statement.
4 Distinguish between 'profit for the year' and 'gross profit'.
5 Describe the term 'working equity'.
6 Outline three uses of a cash budget.

Essential question 5.2

1 **Describe** the purpose of two financial statements.

Ratio analysis

Users of financial statements, such as managers, use a number of ratios to analyse the information they provide.

Ratio analysis is used to:
- compare the performance of the business with previous years
- compare the performance of a business to that of its competitors
- compare against industry averages
- highlight areas of the business that need attention
- highlight trends to aid future decision-making.

Ratio analysis does, however, have **limitations**.
- Ratio information is historical so is not relevant to the current or future position.
- Ratios do not take into account external factors, for example, recessions.
- Ratios do not take into account internal factors, for example, low staff morale.
- Ratios do not take into account product developments.
- It is difficult to find competitors of the *exact* type and size to make valid comparisons.

Profitability ratios

Profitability ratios measure how profitable a business is.

Table 5.9 Profitability ratios

Ratio	Description	How to improve percentage
Gross profit percentage Formula: $\dfrac{\text{gross profit}}{\text{sales revenue}} \times 100$	This measures the *percentage* of profit made from buying and selling. The higher the percentage, the better.	Increase sales revenue, e.g. by changing prices. Switch to a cheaper supplier of purchases.
Profit for the year (net profit) percentage Formula: $\dfrac{\text{profit for the year}}{\text{sales revenue}} \times 100$	This measures the *percentage* of profit made once expenses are deducted from gross profit. The higher the percentage, the better.	Reduce expenses, e.g. lower wage costs by making staff redundant. Increase revenue. Improve gross profit to have a knock-on effect.
Return on capital employed Formula: $\dfrac{\text{profit for the year}}{\text{opening equity}} \times 100$	This measures the *percentage* of investment that is returned to investors such as shareholders. The higher the percentage, the better.	Attempt to increase profit for the year, e.g. by reducing expenses or improving revenue.

Hints & tips

You must use the word 'percentage' when describing profitability ratios. If you don't, you will only be describing a financial term, not a ratio!

Liquidity ratios

Liquidity ratios measure cash situation or the business and its ability to pay its short-term debts.

Table 5.10 Liquidity ratios

Ratio	Description	How to improve percentage
Current ratio Formula: $\dfrac{\text{current assets}}{\text{current liabilities}}$	Measures the ability of a business to pay back short-term debts. The result is expressed as ?:1. Over 2:1 is ideal, as it proves the business has twice the current assets as current liabilities and have a healthy cash flow.	If a business has less than 2:1, they must try and secure more current assets, e.g. by selling non-current assets for cash. They should also reduce current liabilities. If the result is too high, e.g. 4:1 or 5:1, they should invest some current assets.
Acid test ratio Formula: $\dfrac{(\text{current assets} - \text{closing inventory})}{\text{current liabilities}}$	Measures the ability of a business to pay back short-term debts *in a crisis situation*. By removing stock from the equation, the business can assess their cash flow without including the *least liquid* current asset. 1:1 is acceptable.	If a business has less than 1:1, they must secure more current assets, e.g. encouraging cash sales, to improve cash flow. If their current ratio is OK but acid test is too low, it indicates too much money tied up in stock, so they could implement JIT stock control to avoid this.

Efficiency ratios

Efficiency ratios measure how well a business uses their resources.

Table 5.11 Efficiency ratios

Ratio	Description	How to improve percentage
Rate of stock turnover Formula: $$\frac{\text{cost of sales}}{\text{average inventory}^*}$$ $$^*\frac{\text{opening inventory} + \text{closing inventory}}{2}$$	Measures the amount of times a business re-stocks their inventory during the year. The result is expressed in times, e.g. 9 times would indicate a business sold all their stock and ordered more, 9 times in the year.	Most businesses want a high figure as it indicates that stock is selling well and money is not tied up in stock. If the result is too low they should use JIT to avoid overstocking, sell off excess stock or perhaps negotiate sale or return with suppliers (see page 117).

Example 5.4

The following are extracts from the financial statements of Edgar Ltd.

The performance is interpreted by calculating the following ratios:
- gross profit percentage
- current ratio
- acid test ratio.

Extract from income statement for Edgar Ltd				
	Year 1		Year 2	
	£	£	£	£
Sales revenue (Sales)		5000		5200
Less Cost of sales				
Opening inventory (Stock)	500		300	
Add Purchases	2000		2800	
	2500		3100	
Less Closing inventory (Stock)	300		200	
Cost of sales		2200		2900
Gross profit		2800		2300
Less Expenses		1500		1800
Profit for the year (Net profit)		1300		500

Extract from statement of financial position for Edgar Ltd				
	Year 1		Year 2	
	£	£	£	£
Non-current assets (Fixed assets)		10 500		10 400
Add Current assets				
Closing inventory (Stock)	300		200	
Cash	1300		900	
	1600		1100	
Less Current liabilities (Overdraft)	800		1000	
Working capital		800		100
Net assets		11 300		10 500
Equity				
Opening capital	10 000		10 000	
Profit for the year	1300	11 300	500	10 500

Ratio		Interpretation	How to improve
Gross profit percentage			
Change for Year 1 GP / Revenue × 100 = 2800/5000 × 100 = 56%	Change for Year 2 GP / Revenue x 100 = 2300/5200 × 100 = 44%	Year 2 shows a falling GP percentage from Year 1. At first glance, revenue has improved; however, cost of sales has increased, leading to a lower gross profit percentage.	Increase sales revenue by increasing selling prices. Find a cheaper supplier of purchases.
Current ratio			
Year 1 CA / CL = 1600/800 = 2 = 2:1	Year 2 CA / CL = 1100/1000 = 1.1 = 1.1:1	Year 2 shows a falling current ratio. In Year 1 the business has an acceptable result of 2:1. In Year 2 they just cover their current liabilities with their current assets.	Increase the amount of current assets in the business, e.g. cash. Lower the amount of current liabilities in the business, e.g. pay off the overdraft.
Acid test ratio			
Year 1 (CA-CI) / CL = 1600 − 300/CL = 1300/800 = 1.63 = 1.63:1	Year 2 (CA-CI) / CL = 1100 − 200/CL = 900/1000 = 0.9 = 0.9:1	Year 2 shows a falling acid test ratio. In Year 1 the business has a very acceptable result of 1.63:1. In Year 2 a result of 0.9:1 suggests that it is not able to pay off short-term debts in a crisis as stock.	Ensure stock isn't relied on to boost current assets by using JIT. Increase the amount of current assets in the business, e.g. cash.

Case study 5.4
Amber & Saffi Ltd

The Accounting Department of Amber & Saffi Ltd has provided you with ratio analysis results.

Study the information and attempt the discussion points below.

Ratio	Amber & Saffi Ltd	Competitor
Gross profit ratio	45%	68%
Current ratio	5:1	2.5:1
Acid test ratio	0.95:1	1.4:1
Rate of inventory turnover	3 times	6 times
Return on equity employed	25%	20%

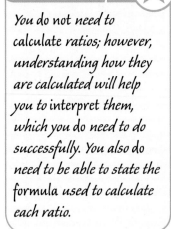

Hints & tips ⭐

You do not need to calculate ratios; however, understanding how they are calculated will help you to interpret them, which you do need to do successfully. You also do need to be able to state the formula used to calculate each ratio.

Discussion points

In pairs, groups or on your own:

1 Identify three areas where the competition is performing better than Amber & Saffi Ltd.
2 Suggest ways for Amber & Saffi Ltd to improve the areas identified in the previous question.
3 Identify one area where Amber & Saffi Ltd are performing better that the competition.
4 Explain the reason for Amber & Saffi Ltd's current ratio figure being so high.

1 Describe the following:
   a) liquidity ratios
   b) profitability ratios
   c) efficiency ratios.
2 Identify a ratio that could be used by potential investors.
3 State the formula for the ratio identified in the previous question.

Essential questions 5.3

1 **Describe** a ratio for each of the categories in key question 1.
2 **Describe** two uses and two limitations of ratio analysis.

Activity 5.1

Practicing preparing financial statements, while not required to pass the Higher Business Management course, is a good way to understand them, so you can develop skills in how to interpret them.

1 Using a spreadsheet package, such as Microsoft Excel, enter the following information to create an **Income Statement** and a **Statement of Financial Position**.
2 The figures that you need are in the table below, you aren't required to calculate them, however it will help you understand the benefits of using a spreadsheet package if you try to enter formula to calculate them for you. Ask your teacher for help with this.
3 Use the examples in this chapter to help you enter each figure and term correctly.

	£		£
Sales revenue	4725	Profit for the year	3000
Opening inventory	225	Non-current assets	3500
Purchases	725	Cash	975
Closing inventory	300	Bank overdraft	325
Cost of sales	**650**	Trade payables	450
Gross profit	**4075**	**Working equity**	**500**
Rent	500	**Net assets**	**4000**
Wages	575	Share capital	1000

Use of technology in managing finance

Here is a summary of how technology can be used in the finance department.

- Spreadsheets can be used to prepare financial statements. This allows:
  - greater accuracy using formula, reducing the margin for error
  - formula can be replicated, saving time
  - 'What if?' statements can be used to forecast the outcome of different scenarios
  - charts and graphs can be made easily, allowing the information to be analysed and presented.
- Presentation software can be used to engage audiences when presenting information through the use of animations and colour.
- Email can be used to circulate financial information quickly.
- Local area networks (LAN) can be used to share documents so that different employees can assess and share information.

Exam-style questions practice – Chapter 5

1 Explain the ways a business can overcome cash flow problems. (**5 marks**)
2 Describe the financial statements a business can use to assess its performance. (**4 marks**)
3 Distinguish between the following:
   a) debentures and shares
   b) current ratio and acid test ratio. (**4 marks**)
4 Describe the role of a manager in the Finance Department. (**5 marks**)
5 a) Describe the limitations of ratio analysis, apart from information being historical. (**3 marks**)
   b) The accounting department of ESQ Ltd has calculated information using ratios and the following results were provided:

Ratio	ESQ Ltd	Competitor
Gross profit ratio	17%	29%
Current ratio	6.8:1	2.3:1

Explain the actions required by ESQ Ltd to improve each figure in order to be more competitive. (**4 marks**)

Chapter 6

Outcome 3.1: Management of Marketing

Management of marketing

It is the role of the Marketing department to anticipate, identify and satisfy the needs and wants of customers.

Customers

Marketing aims to raise customer awareness of their products. The level to which they try and meet the needs of customers will depend on whether the business is **market led** or **product led**.

Market or product led?

Table 6.1 Characteristics of market-led and product-led businesses

Market led	Product led
The business develops products based on customer wants.	The business produces products that they believe customers will want and try to convince them to buy them.
High levels of market research carried out to determine customer wants.	Market research is not seen as important. There are, however, high levels of product research and development.
Market-led businesses often exist in highly competitive markets.	New technologies, with little to no competition, are often product led.
The marketing mix will be responsive to changes in external factors and consumer behaviour.	Often the product is unresponsive to changing external factors.

Consumer behaviour

Businesses, especially market-led businesses, need to take account of **consumer behaviour**. Consumer behaviour is the thoughts consumers have and the actions they take when purchasing products.

In order to satisfy consumers' needs and wants, the market-led business needs to understand why, what, how and where consumers buy products.

Table 6.2 Understanding the why, what, how and where of consumer behaviour

Consumer behaviour	Description	Impact on market-led business
Why do consumers buy products?	Need/want, social status, gift for someone else?	Businesses need to understand the different motivations customers have and offer products accordingly. This is linked to Maslow's hierarchy (see page 55), i.e. some purchases are for basic needs e.g. food, others are for self-actualisation needs, e.g. a Rolex watch.
What types of purchases do consumers make?	Routine buying, e.g. food or fuel. Impulse buying just because it caught their eye? Extensive decision-making purchases, e.g. a new car.	Marketing has to raise awareness of products. Promotion methods, such as sales promotions or advertising, can influence routine purchases. Point of sale merchandising materials, for example, displays, can influence impulse buying.
How do consumers purchase products?	Do consumers pay with: <ul><li>cash/debit card</li><li>credit card</li><li>store credit etc.?</li></ul>	A business needs to be responsive to changes in how consumers wish to purchase products, for example, the move to a cashless society and the introduction of contactless card payments is a result of the need for convenience due to lifestyle changes.
Where do consumers purchase products?	Retail outlets? E-commerce? Catalogues?	Businesses need to adapt and sell products in ways that are responsive to changes in consumer behaviour. There has been a massive growth in e-commerce, again due to the need for convenience.

Market research

Market research is essential in order to anticipate and identify customers' needs and wants, especially for market-led businesses. There are two main types of market research, **field research** and **desk research**. Each has advantages and disadvantages:

Table 6.3 Advantages and disadvantages of different types of research

Type of research	Advantages	Disadvantages
Desk research: Involves researching and analysing information that has already been gathered. Examples include looking at: <ul><li>web pages (perhaps to find out competitor prices)</li><li>trade magazines</li><li>government publications</li><li>financial statements</li><li>sales figures</li><li>previous market research reports.</li></ul>	Timely – desk information is quick to gather. Cost effective – desk information does not require trained and paid interviewers or research companies. Available – desk information already exists so is easy to look up.	Not objective – desk information is collected and presented by someone else, so could be biased. Not appropriate – desk information is not fit for the *exact* purpose and may have to be 'shoehorned' to fit the business' needs. Not concise – the researcher may have to read through a lot of information to get what is needed.

Field research:		
Involves gathering brand new information suitable for the business' exact needs. Examples are explored in depth in this chapter.	Complete – field information should have no parts missing. Timely – in the respect that the information is up to date. Appropriate – field information is fit for the purpose it is needed for. Accurate – information should be correct as it can be validated.	Not cost effective – field information requires trained and paid interviewers or expensive research companies.

Remember

... the costs and benefits of research methods with the fun mnemonic TAAACCCO (an overstuffed taco!). Use these along with the specific benefits of field research for your coursework assignment!

Field research

Sampling

Every potential customer of a business' product is known as the **population**. Table 6.4 shows the methods of **sampling**, selecting people from that population to conduct market research on, that can be used.

Table 6.4 Advantages and disadvantages of different types of sampling

Sampling method	Advantages	Disadvantages
Random sampling: The sample is picked randomly, e.g. using a telephone directory or list of customers.	No bias is shown by the researcher. Saves time in selecting the sample.	Sample may not reflect the target market. Can over represent a certain segment, e.g. all males could be chosen at random. Can be expensive as many calls may have to be made if customer lists are not up to date.
Quota sampling: The researcher chooses from a group of people with certain characteristics.	Quick and easy method as group lists are pre-made.	The exact sample from each group is not randomised, so researcher bias could be involved.
Stratified random sampling: A sample is selected that is representative of the target market, e.g. if 75% of the population for a product is working class, male and aged 20–30, then that's what 75% of the sample should be.	Sample represents the target market. No researcher bias as the sample is randomised from the list of those that meet the characteristics required.	Takes time to work through population lists and select the exact sample required. The sample chosen could be geographically dispersed, adding to the costs of research.
Cluster sampling: The population is split into smaller 'clusters', often geographically, which could represent the population on a small scale.	Saves time compared to researching samples spread across wider areas. One of the cheapest methods of sampling.	Risk of the sample not being accurate enough to represent the target market.

Methods of field research

Once a sample population has been identified, the filed research method must be chosen.

Table 6.5 Advantages and disadvantages of different types of field research

Method	Advantages	Disadvantages
Telephone survey: A market researcher telephones customers, usually at home, and asks them questions.	Easy to target specific customers, e.g. calling 0141 numbers to target customers living in Glasgow, to allow local needs to be met. Information is obtained immediately and can be clarified if necessary.	Customers can feel that telephone surveys are intrusive and may not wish to respond. Only short surveys can be carried out.
Postal survey: A survey is sent to customers through the post and is returned once completed.	Easy to target specific customers, e.g. sending out surveys on exclusive products to affluent postcodes, to meet the needs of specific segments. Customers can choose to complete the survey at a time that is most convenient to them.	Questions must be simple and easy to follow for the best result. Customers often view postal surveys as 'junk mail' and will simply ignore them.
Online survey: A website or email is used to ask customers questions.	Customers can be surveyed across a very large geographical area. Online software can often be used to collate and analyse the results easily.	The responses may be too brief to be meaningful, as clarification cannot be gained. Access to the internet must be available.
Personal interview: Often conducted as a street survey or by 'cold calling' at customers' homes.	Allows two-way communication. The interviewer can respond to the customer's body language, tone of voice and facial expression to encourage fuller responses.	It can take a lot of time to conduct the interviews. Customers may feel that this sort of questioning is a nuisance and may not wish to respond.
Hall tests: A product is given to customers to try and their feedback is gathered.	Good quality feedback can be gathered based on the product trial, allowing changes to be made. Inexpensive and easy to do.	Customers' opinions and feelings can be more difficult to analyse. Customers might feel they need to give a positive response as they have been given a free product.
Focus groups: A group of customers is brought together and asked to answer and discuss questions put forward by a market researcher.	More in-depth feedback can be gathered. Customers have agreed to participate so considered responses are more likely.	Customers' opinions and feelings can be more difficult to analyse. Strong personalities within the group can sway discussion and opinion.
Consumer audit: Used by large market research companies to continuously monitor customer habits and influences. One means of auditing is to ask some customers to record their responses to products they have purchased.	As the information is gathered over a period of time, customer trends can be identified. More detailed feedback can be gathered on products and so shape future changes.	Participants receive payment so this method can be expensive. Information recorded may be inaccurate or incomplete, and therefore unhelpful.

Test marketing:		
A new product is launched in a regional area and the reaction is monitored. Successful products are then launched to a wider market.	Changes can be made to products before they are launched to a wider market. Money can be saved on launching a product to a wider market if it is unsuccessful in the test area.	Customers in one area may have tastes that are not representative of the wider market.
Electronic point of sale (EPOS):		
Information on customer preferences and habits is gathered as their loyalty cards are swiped through electronic tills. Used in conjunction with loyalty schemes to match purchasing information with customer details.	Gathers vital information about consumer behaviour, such as when they buy, what they buy, how they react to promotions or price changes, which can allow an effective marketing mix to be formed and stock ordered accordingly. Allows retailers to offer promotions, for example, money-off coupons, tailored to the individual customer's actual needs and preferences.	It can be very expensive to set up the systems. It can be time consuming to set up. When used with loyalty schemes, reward points lead to money-off vouchers which lower potential profits for the business. Information can be incomplete if customers decide to shop elsewhere at times.

www

You will need to use field research methods to complete your coursework assignment. Take a look at: **www.surveymonkey.com**. It's free!

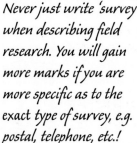

Hints & tips

Never just write 'survey' when describing field research. You will gain more marks if you are more specific as to the exact type of survey, e.g. postal, telephone, etc.!

Key questions 6.1

1 a) Outline two types of consumer behaviour.
   b) Describe the impact on businesses of the behaviour you mentioned in question 1a.
2 Describe three methods of sampling.
3 Discuss one advantage and one disadvantage of using EPOS for market research purposes.

Essential question 6.1

Explain two ways market research can be used to enhance the effectiveness of a large organisation.

Marketing mix

The marketing mix is the combination of **product**, **price**, **place**, **promotion**, **people**, **process** and **physical evidence** that makes the marketing of a product successful.

Product

Product refers to *what* a business sells. A product can be either a **good** or a **service**.

Remember

It should be easy to remember the marketing mix — they all begin with the letter 'P'. Just remember that at N5 level Business Management you only had to know the '4Ps'; at Higher level you need to know the '7Ps'!

Product life cycle

All products have a life cycle. Some products go through the stages of a life cycle very quickly, known as **fads**, while others can have a life cycle that lasts many decades, for example, Coca Cola. The stages of the product life cycle are shown in Figure 6.1.

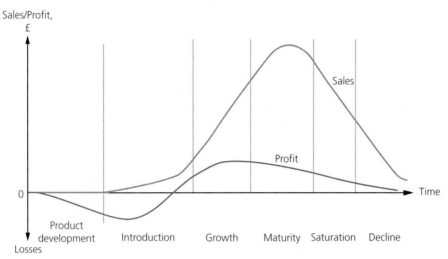

Figure 6.1 The product life cycle.

Table 6.6 Stages of the product life cycle and each stage's impact on sales and profits

Stage	Impact on sales	Impact on profits
Development: The product is being researched and developed. Prototypes will be made and tested. Changes may have to be made after research feedback.	There are no sales yet as the product is still being developed.	The product will actually be making a loss due to the costs of development and zero income from sales.
Introduction: The product is launched. This usually coincides with introductory promotional activities to create 'hype' for the product.	Sales are slow to begin with as customers are unsure of the product. Customers may have to be persuaded to move from competitor products.	The product begins to cut into the losses from development, but high promotional costs still result in a loss being made overall.
Growth: The product has been on the market for some time, customers are fully aware of the product and are purchasing it.	Sales start to rise rapidly. This can be the result of slightly reduced prices, lack of competition and/or consumer confidence in the product.	Profits are starting to be made and losses from development and promotions during the initial stages are recouped.
Maturity: The product has been on the market for some time. Competition enters the market.	Sales growth peaks and levels out. Many sales can still be made for a long time at this stage.	Profits can still be healthy but start to fall. The competition will take sales away and thus profits will fall.
Saturation: The product suffers from too many competitors being in the market.	Sales begin to fall as consumers flock to competitors' products.	Profits fall rapidly, especially if prices are slashed to encourage sales.
Decline: The product's life is nearing the end. The product will stop being produced.	Sales fall rapidly and eventually the product will be withdrawn from the market.	Profits continue to fall. Eventually products may be sold at unit cost just to break even.

Activity 6.1

You are going to make your own product life cycle diagram!

1. Choose a business or a market as a whole, for example, you could choose Nintendo or the whole computer consoles market.
2. Create a blank product life cycle diagram by copying the X axis and Y axis of Figure 6.1. You can do this on a poster-sized piece of paper or on a computer using publishing software such as Microsoft Publisher.
3. Research your chosen business or market using the internet, newspapers, magazines, etc. and decide which products belong at each stage. Print or cut out images of these products and stick them along your product life cycle!
4. Add in notes to justify why each product belongs at each stage.
5. Present your findings to others, either via PowerPoint presentation or by describing the features of your poster.

Hints & tips ★

*You need to be able to explain the impact of each stage of the product life cycle on **sales** and **profits**.*

Extension strategies

As sales (and profits) begin to fall as a product matures, a business can attempt to inject new life into the product. This is known as **extending the product life cycle**. There are a number of extension strategies a business can use, these are shown in Table 6.7:

Table 6.7 Product life cycle extension strategies

Extension strategy	Impact
Lowering the price of the product, e.g. through a 'sale'	Reducing prices will make the product more affordable and therefore appeal to more market segments.
Changing the place the product is sold, e.g. selling online	Making the product available in more places will mean it is seen by more potential customers, e.g. using e-commerce will mean a product can be sold worldwide.
Altering the methods of promotion	Changing the way a product is promoted can increase sales simply by raising awareness of that product.
Developing variations of the product, e.g. new flavours	Developing new varieties can mean the product appeals to the tastes and desires of different market segments. Updating the product can utilise the latest technology so make customers want the product again, e.g. annual launches of the latest, updated smartphones.
Rebranding the product	Changing the name of the product can create 'hype'. A new name can appeal to different or wider market segments, e.g. Jif changed to Cif as they found that continental Europeans couldn't pronounce Jif!
Changing the packaging	Redesigning the packaging can make the product appeal to a new market segment, e.g. Pepsi changed their logo and the design of cans to make it look more modern and 'cool' to appeal to teenagers.
Changing the use of the product	Extending or changing the use of a product can make it appeal to new markets or suit seasonal tastes , e.g. Cadbury's Minirolls now come in ice-cream-inspired flavours and are suitable for freezing, ideal for summer!

Product portfolio

A business should strive to have a product portfolio. This means having a range of products on sale. There are two types of product portfolio: **product line portfolios** and **diversified product portfolios**.

Product line portfolios

A product line portfolio involves having a variety of similar products on sale. Greater profits can be gained from having so many products on sale as different products 'in the line' will appeal to different market segments with different tastes. For example, Arcadia is a clothing company with brands such as Top Shop, Top Man, Miss Selfridge, and Dorothy Perkins; Arcadia can meet the needs of many different market segments such as males, females, young and old.

Diversified product portfolio

A diversified product portfolio involves having products for sale across completely different market segments. This variety spreads the risk across different markets in case one fails. For example, Virgin, which owns Virgin Bank, still had products to fall back on during the banking crisis, such as Virgin Media and Virgin Atlantic.

Case study 6.1
Nestlé

Nestlé have managed to combine an extensive product line with a diversified product portfolio. They are best known for their range of chocolate bars such as KitKat, Aero and Yorkie but they also have a complete range of cereals including Shreddies, Cheerios and Golden Nuggets, as well as a range of other well-known store cupboard staples such as Nescafe, Nesquik and Nestea. They even own pet food brands such as Purina and Felix!

Figure 6.2 Nestlé's product portfolio.

Discussion points
In pairs, groups or on your own:

1 Discuss examples of Nestlé's product line.
2 Discuss examples of Nestlé's diversified product portfolio.
3 Suggest the market segments that different Nestlé products appeal to.

Boston matrix

Businesses can analyse their product portfolio using a **Boston matrix**. This enables products to be analysed on two fronts:

1 **market share** – the percentage of sales in the market a product makes.
2 **market growth** – the overall potential for sales that the market has as a whole.

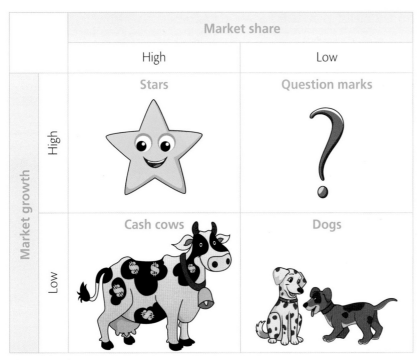

Figure 6.3 The Boston matrix.

Table 6.8 Boston matrix product types

Product type	Impact
Stars: Products that have a high market share in a high-growth market, e.g. Apple's iPad.	Stars need constant investment in marketing to keep ahead in a competitive market. Stars allow a business to be a market leader. Over time, stars will decline into either question marks or cash cows (see below).
Cash cows: Products that have a high market share of a low-growth market, e.g. Microsoft's Office software.	Cash cows should require little marketing expense due to lack of competition. Funds generated can be used to further strengthen stars and improve riskier ventures, such as question marks.
Question marks/Problem children: Products that have a low market share in a market with high growth potential, e.g. manufacturers of less popular brands of tablet computers.	Question marks can be invested in due to their position in a promising market. They need development of a strong marketing mix if they are to be turned into stars.
Dogs: Products that have a low market share of a market with low growth, e.g. less popular brands in declining technology industries.	Dogs can adversely affect profits. Dogs should be divested due to the lack of market share and the declining market for the product. They cannot be turned into stars.

Advantages and disadvantages of a product portfolio

Table 6.9 Advantages and disadvantages of a product portfolio

Advantages	Disadvantages
Businesses can spread risk over different markets.	There are high costs involved in researching and developing so many products.
A business can meet the needs of different market segments and appeal to more customers.	High marketing costs are incurred to promote so many products.
Newer products can replace those at the end of their life cycle.	Bad publicity surrounding one product can affect the whole portfolio.
A range of products increases the awareness of the brand as a whole.	Resources assigned to new products may affect the performance of existing products.
A business will find it easier to launch new products with a large existing portfolio.	Dogs can drain a business of profits unless they are divested.
Cash cows can fund other, riskier, ventures such as the marketing of stars.	
Stars allow a business to be market leader in one area which will improve the brand image overall.	
Question mark products give businesses an opportunity to invest and grow.	
Dogs can be divested to reduce losses.	

Activity 6.2

You are going to create your own Boston matrix.

1 Choose a business or a market as a whole, for example you could choose Apple or the whole mobile phone market.
2 Create a blank Boston matrix by copying Figure 6.5. You can do this on a poster-sized piece of paper or on a computer using publishing software.
3 Research your chosen company or market using the internet or newspapers and decide which products belong in each box. Print or cut out products and stick them onto your Boston matrix.
4 Add notes justifying why each product belongs in each box.
5 Present your findings to others, either via PowerPoint presentation or by describing the features of your poster.

Price

Pricing strategies

There are a number of different pricing strategies that can be used by businesses. A business will use different pricing strategies for different products in their portfolio.

Table 6.10 Advantages and disadvantages of different pricing strategies

Pricing strategy	Advantages	Disadvantages
Cost plus: The business calculates the unit cost of a product and then adds a percentage mark up for profit, e.g. it costs PC World £300 to purchase a laptop which they then mark up by 50% and sell to the customer for £450.	A quick and easy way of setting the selling price. Ensures that total costs are covered and a profit is generated.	Doesn't cover indirect costs, e.g. other expenses such as rent. Doesn't take external factors into account, e.g. increasing prices during boom periods to maximise profits.
Competitive: The price of a product is set similar to the competitors, e.g., fuel prices.	Avoids a price war. Encourages competition, which improves the market as a whole.	Other elements of the marketing mix must be better than the competition's to ensure sales.
Skimming: The price is set high to begin with and lowers over time, e.g. with electronics, such as the iPad, PS4, etc.	Sufficient 'hype' around a new product enables higher prices to be charged, which can increase profits. Lack of competition also allows maximum prices to be charged.	High initial prices can put off some customers. Technique results in low initial sales numbers.
Penetration: The price is set low to begin with and increases over time, e.g. 'trial prices' on new chocolate bars.	Encourages customers to try a new product. The business hopes to gain repeat custom once the price rises.	Very little profit can be generated during the initial low price period.
Price discrimination: Prices are altered depending on a discriminating factor, e.g. different prices are often charged in the transport industries depending on age, such as a child price, adult price and senior citizen price.	Ensures products appeal to different market segments. Allows for high profit margins on some price brackets.	Harder to budget for sales revenue in advance.
Destroyer: The price is deliberately set extremely low for a period of time to force out competitors.	Competitors are forced out of the market, then prices can increase again. Increases market share.	Can only be used by larger companies that can afford to make losses while prices are low. Could breach CMA's anti-competition regulations (see page 39).
Loss leaders: The price of some products is set unprofitably low to entice customers in to buy other products.	Creates greater footfall, i.e. brings customers to the business. Hopefully, customers will buy normal-priced products while buying loss leaders. Encourages repeat purchases.	There is a risk that some customers will only buy the loss leaders, impacting on profits.
Premium: The price is permanently set higher than that of the competition, e.g. Mulberry bags.	This creates an image of quality and exclusivity. Some customers are attracted to the prestige of high prices.	Customers looking for value for money will go elsewhere.

Low:		
The price is permanently set lower than that of the competition, e.g. Primark.	This attracts customers looking for value for money. High volume of sales.	Some customers are put off by low prices as they believe it indicates low quality.
Demand pricing:		
The price is set in line with the economic laws of **supply and demand**. (This law dictates that high demand leads to higher prices, while low demand leads to lower prices.)	The business ensures that the price charged is what customers are prepared to pay. This is known as the 'equilibrium price'. When demand is low it ensures that some sales are encouraged due to the low price.	Businesses need to employ effective research methods to establish demand levels. The price needs to be constantly recalculated and changed.

Factors affecting pricing strategy

Table 6.11 contains factors that can affect the pricing strategy chosen.

Table 6.11 Factors affecting the pricing strategy chosen

Factor	Description
Target market for the product	Mass-market products need to be priced in a way that will appeal to most income segments, whereas exclusive products aimed at wealthy segments can be priced higher.
Demand for the product	If the demand for a product is high, then the business can maximise profits by setting the price high; once demand drops, they can lower the price to encourage sales, e.g. the most popular Christmas toy each year is always in high demand, so sells for a high price. 'January sales' are a result of demand dropping after the Christmas rush.
Objectives of the business	If the objective is to maximise sales, a lower price might be offered. If the objective is to maximise profits, a higher price may be set.
External factors	Prices should be lowered during a recession to encourage sales or increased during boom periods to maximise profits. Similarly, prices may have to be lowered to respond to the prices offered by competitors.
Cost of the product	Any pricing strategy should take into account the cost to produce the product (unit cost) as well as other costs that need to be covered, such as rent. For this reason, loss leaders and destroyer pricing should be used sparingly and for short periods.

Activity 6.3

Finding real and current examples of pricing strategies will help you remember them, so, you are going to make your own 'prices scrapbook'.

1 Use the internet, newspapers, catalogues or promotional materials to find examples of a product for each pricing strategy.
2 Print or cut out and stick a picture of each product onto a poster, blank booklet or your jotter, or copy and paste images onto a blank document in a word-processing or desktop publishing package on your computer.
3 Describe each pricing strategy beside each product example; be sure to give advantages and disadvantages.
4 Present your findings to others and make sure you keep your finished work to help you revise pricing strategies later.

Place

Channels of distribution

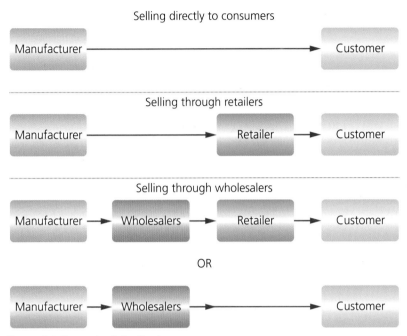

Figure 6.4 Channels of distribution.

Channels of distribution are the possible routes taken by a product to reach the consumer from the manufacturer.

Factors affecting the channel of distribution

Table 6.12 shows factors that can affect the channel of distribution that is chosen by a business for a particular product.

Table 6.12 Factors affecting channels of distribution

Factor	Description
Finance available	A manufacturer may not have the finance available to set up e-commerce or print catalogues to sell direct, so using wholesalers or retailers are the only options.
Desired image for the product	Certain products have images that dictate where they can be sold, e.g. Hugo Boss only sell in retailers that have built up a good reputation over at least 5 years.
Shelf life of the product	Some products need to be shipped to retailers fast as they will go out of date quickly, e.g. fresh fruit.
Legal restrictions	Some products can't be sold through certain channels, e.g. prescription medicines need to be sold through pharmacists.
Stage of the product life cycle	Products may only be sold in exclusive outlets at the beginning of a product's life cycle, but may be sold in discount stores during their decline stage to encourage sales.
Technical qualities of the product	Highly technical products may need to be demonstrated, which means personal selling is the ideal channel.

Direct selling
Direct selling means selling direct to the consumer from the manufacturer.
This is the shortest channel of distribution and means there are less 'middle men' taking a cut of the profits. Businesses also retain control of *how* their product is marketed.

Table 6.13 contains methods of direct selling that a business could use.

Table 6.13 Advantages and disadvantages of different methods of direct selling

Method	Advantages	Disadvantages
E-commerce: A business sells its products using the internet, e.g. ASOS.	Customers in the global market can be reached, 24/7. An entire range can be shown online. Online discounts can be offered to attract customers. Product information and customer comments can sway purchasing decisions.	It can take a lot of time and expense to design attractive, high-quality websites. Customers might be wary of providing their personal details online. Customers need to have access to the internet. Customers need to wait for products to arrive and may have to pay delivery costs.
Mail order: A business sells its products using a catalogue, which is usually sent directly to the customer, e.g. M and M Direct.	Credit facilities are often offered to customers. Customers can browse for products and place orders from home, at a time that suits them. Mail-order-only companies save money on staffing and store costs.	Glossy catalogues can be expensive to produce. Producing catalogues is not environmentally friendly and may not meet CSR aims (see page 10). A level of bad debt might be incurred.
Direct mail: A business posts letters, leaflets and brochures directly to the customer.	Specific market segments can be targeted, e.g. by inserting supermarket recipe cards inside cookery magazines. A wide geographical area can be targeted by placing leaflets inside newspapers and magazines.	Customers can perceive this as 'junk mail' and simply throw it away. Customer mailing lists can quickly become out of date, meaning a business may target the wrong people and waste money.
Personal selling: A salesperson sells products directly to the customer, often by going 'door to door' or over the phone (telesales).	Allows a demonstration or explanation of the product to be given. Feedback on products can be gathered from customers.	Customers can find this type of selling a nuisance and may not be keen to listen. Staffing costs and commission make this method expensive and increasingly unpopular with businesses.
Online shopping channels: A business sells products on the TV using dedicated shopping channels, e.g. QVC.	Customers can see products being modelled and demonstrated. Customers can be encouraged to buy on impulse due to short-term bargain prices.	Customers need to switch on to the channel before they can be targeted. Customers need to wait for products to arrive and may have to pay delivery costs.

Retailers

Manufacturers selling products through a **retailer** have the following advantages and disadvantages:

Table 6.14 Advantages and disadvantages of selling through a retailer

Advantages	Disadvantages
Retailers are located close to customers.	Retailers take a cut of the profits.
Retailers often promote the product for the manufacturer.	Retailers may alter the price of the product and so have an effect on the image of the product.
Retailers employ sales assistants to help sell the product.	The product will face competition from other products stocked by the retailer.
Larger retailers buy in bulk.	

Trends in retailer types

The different retailer types have changed in recent years as Table 6.15 illustrates.

Table 6.15 Advantages and disadvantages of different types of retailer

Retailer type	Advantages	Disadvantages
Hypermarkets and superstores: There has been a growth in massive supermarkets, which sell many goods and services under one roof. The largest of these are known as Hypermarkets e.g. Tesco Extra.	Most hypermarkets open 24/7. A huge range of products are offered to customers.	Lack of competition from high-street stores can lead to poorer quality products.
Convenience supermarkets: Due to changing work patterns and lifestyle changes, there has been a growth in smaller supermarkets appearing in convenient locations, such as M&S Simply Food or Little Waitrose in city centres, near transport hubs or on forecourts.	Cater for the changing needs of customers so are guaranteed footfall. Prices can be slightly higher than larger supermarkets due to the convenience factor.	Limited choice of products due to smaller store sizes. There can be high levels of waste as it is harder to predict customer numbers than it is for larger, more traditional supermarkets.
Out-of-town retail parks: Out-of-town (OOT) retailing is now found on the outskirts of most major towns in the UK, with good infrastructure such as road links and free car parking, e.g. Glasgow Fort.	Infrastructure attracts customers. Often near amenities such as restaurant chains and cinemas, which can increase footfall. Larger store sizes mean a good product range for low prices due to bulk buying by OOT retailers.	Limited choice of stores compared to high-street shopping or more traditional shopping malls. Only suitable for customers with access to transport.
Online retailers: Amazon is the biggest online retailer (dubbed 'e-tailer') in the UK. Rather than setting up their own e-commerce site, some manufacturers will sell through retailers like this.	Products can be sold to a world-wide market by online retailers. Products can be sold 24/7.	Customers can't try or touch the product before buying. Delivery charges may put some customers off.
Discount stores: In response to the recession, discount stores have become popular in the UK over the last few years, e.g. Poundland and B&M Homestores.	Products are sold for rock-bottom prices, which attracts customers looking for value.	Limited product range compared to other retailers. Some customers don't like the image of discount stores.

Case study 6.2
Supermarket wars!

The big four supermarkets in the UK have been adapting the types of retail outlet they offer customers over the past few years. Tesco, the market leader in the UK, has many 'Tesco Superstores' and 'Tesco Extra' branded hypermarkets as well as 'Tesco Metro' and 'Tesco Express' convenience supermarkets.

Sainsbury's, on the other hand, do not have a specific hypermarket brand, but many of their larger stores are the same size as competing Tesco hypermarkets. However, Sainsbury's do offer 'Sainsbury's Local' convenience supermarkets and have recently announced they are launching discount store 'Netto' in the UK.

Meanwhile, Morrison's convenience supermarket is called Morrison's M Local while ASDA currently only have one ASDA Essentials convenience supermarket in the UK. Smaller supermarket chains such as Waitrose and M&S have also recently joined the trend for setting up convenience supermarkets in city centres, train stations and petrol station forecourts, called Little Waitrose and M&S Simply Food respectively.

Figure 6.5 Two of the 'Big 4' supermarkets in the UK – Tesco and Sainsbury's.

Discussion points

In pairs, groups or on your own:

1 Suggest reasons for Tesco having such a vast range of stores.
2 Explain why Sainsbury's are launching the discount store, Netto.

---

www 🖱

Visit **www.googleearth.com** to find different types of retailers in your town. Print out images and add them to your notes to aid your revision of this topic.

Wholesalers

Manufacturers can sell goods to **wholesalers** to distribute to smaller retailers or, direct to customers. Using a wholesaler has the following advantages and disadvantages for *manufacturers*:

Table 6.16 Advantages and disadvantages for manufacturers of using a wholesaler

Advantages for manufacturers	Disadvantages for manufacturers
Packaging and displaying of goods is carried out by the wholesaler, saving the manufacturer time and costs.	Manufacturers make less profit as a cut is taken by wholesalers.
Wholesalers buy in bulk, saving manufacturers from making lots of smaller deliveries.	The manufacturer loses control of how the product is marketed.
Wholesalers can promote products to retailers, which saves the manufacturer promotion costs.	The manufacturer loses control of which retailers the product is sold to.
The wholesaler carries the risk of products going out of fashion as manufacturers get rid of stock as soon it is produced.	

There are also advantages and disadvantages of using a wholesaler for *retailers*:

Table 6.17 Advantages and disadvantages for retailers of using a wholesaler

Advantages for retailers	Disadvantages for retailers
Retailers can save on storage facilities by buying smaller quantities from wholesalers than they would get from manufacturers.	It is more expensive than going directly to manufacturers as wholesalers add on a margin of profit.
Retailers can benefit from promotions offered by wholesalers that they may not get direct from manufacturers.	Wholesalers offer the same products to retailers' competitors, so other areas of the marketing mix have to be relied on.
Retailers can trial smaller orders of newer products and not be left with large amounts of unsold stock.	The retailer may miss out on exclusivity deals by not going direct to manufacturers.

Promotion

Promotion is the process of raising awareness of products and persuading customers to buy them instead of going to competitors. Promotions can be split into two categories, **above the line** and **below the line**.

Above-the-line promotion

Promotions that are said to be '**above the line**' (ATL) use mass media to convey messages to consumers.

Table 6.18 Advantages and disadvantages of above-the-line promotion methods

Advantages	Disadvantages
Often advertisement design is outsourced to advertising agencies meaning high quality adverts.	The business doesn't have direct *control* over which consumers their products are advertised too.
Adverts can reach very wide audiences across many market segments.	Above the line is very expensive due to paying for adverts to be produced by experts and for the mass media to carry them.

The following are examples of types of media that businesses can use:

Table 6.19 Different types of media and their advantages and disadvantages

Advertising media	Advantages	Disadvantages
TV: Advertising products during commercial breaks or sponsoring programmes.	Colour, sound and movement can be used to appeal to customers. Adverts can be used to target a large national audience covering all market segments or specific segments during certain programmes.	Some customers may 'channel hop' to avoid watching adverts. It can be very expensive, especially for prime-time slots. The product may not need to be advertised to all market segments on national TV.
Commercial radio: Advertising during commercial breaks or sponsoring radio programmes.	A more captive audience than TV as listeners don't tend to channel hop, especially in cars. Use of jingles and sound can make adverts memorable.	No images or pictures make products hard to demonstrate.

Newspapers:		
Advertising spaces or full page spreads can be used.	Customers across a large geographical area can be reached. Specific market segments can be targeted by advertising in the correct paper, e.g. local papers for local products or high-quality Sunday papers for exclusive products.	Adverts are often in black and white, with no sound or movement. It can be expensive to advertise in national newspapers.
Magazines:		
Advertising spaces or full page spreads can be used.	Adverts appear in colour, which improves impact. These can target specific market segments based on magazine type. Magazines are often kept for future reference.	It can be expensive, especially for well-known magazines. Competitors will often advertise in the same publications.
Cinema:		
Advertising products while the audience is waiting for the film to begin.	Offers a captive audience as customers can't switch channel! Specific market segments based on film type can be targeted, e.g. toys are advertised before Disney films. Adverts can be enhanced with surround sound and 3D effects.	Customers only see the advert once and cannot choose to replay it. Some customers purposely arrive late to avoid the commercials. Customers tend to remember the film rather than the advertisements.
Internet:		
Advertising products on websites as pop ups and ad banners.	Relatively cheap. This can target specific market segments based on browsing history and 'cookies'.	Some customers ignore this type of advert. Pop-up blockers can prevent customers from viewing adverts.
Digital screens:		
Advertising products in public places in the form of moving images.	Colour, sound and movement can be used for impact. It can be viewed by a large audience in busy areas. More frequently being used to advertise in previously unused spaces, e.g. escalators and lifts.	It can be expensive for city-centre locations or in large sports stadiums. It may begin to be viewed as part of the scenery and be ignored.
Billboards:		
Advertising products in public places in the form of posters and still images.	It can be viewed by a large audience in busy areas. As it is fixed for a period of time people will see it many times.	These are often vandalised, which can give the product a poor image. The quality of the poster can be affected by the weather.

Below-the-line promotion

Promotions that are said to be '**below the line**' (BTL) do not use mass media.

Table 6.20 Advantages and disadvantages of below-the-line promotion methods

Advantages	Disadvantages
Businesses have more control over the customers that adverts are aimed at.	The impact can often only last for a limited period, e.g. a social media post on a business' social media page.
BTL is more affordable than ATL so is more suitable for smaller businesses.	Some customers dislike BTL methods as they are intrusive, e.g. direct mailing.

Sales promotions

The most straightforward of the below-the-line promotions are **sales promotions**. Sales promotions are used for the following reasons:

- to help launch a new product into a competitive market
- as **extension strategies** at the end of a product's life cycle
- to prise customers away from competitors
- to reward existing customers so they stay loyal.

Sales promotions can be either into the pipeline or out of the pipeline.

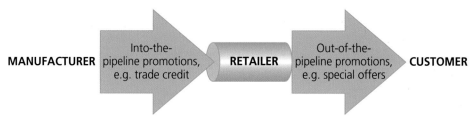

Figure 6.6 Into- and out-of-the-pipeline sales promotions.

Into-the-pipeline sales promotions are offered by the *manufacturer* to encourage *retailers* to purchase products from them.

Table 6.21 Into-the-pipeline sales promotions methods, with advantages and disadvantages

Method	Advantages	Disadvantages
Trade credit: Manufacturers offer retailers credit to pay for goods at a later date.	Retailers can purchase stock and then pay for it once it is sold.	This could lead to bad debt if retailers are unable to sell stock.
Merchandising materials: Free posters and display materials are given to retailers to display products to customers.	This can enhance the look of the retail store.	Retailers may need to dispose of bulky display materials at the end of the promotion.
Sale or return: Manufacturers give retailers the option to return stock that does not sell.	It allows retailers to try new products without the risk of being stuck with unsold stock.	Products may be returned in a poor condition, creating waste.
Bulk-buying discounts: Discounts used to encourage retailers to stock up on a product, e.g. buy one, get one free.	Retailers can save on the unit cost of products, allowing for greater profits.	Retailers may overstock and find they are unable to sell. Products might go out of date or out of fashion.

Out-of-the-pipeline sales promotions are offered by the *retailer* to encourage *customers* to purchase products from them.

Table 6.22 Out-of-the-pipeline sales promotions methods, with advantages and disadvantages

Method	Advantages	Disadvantages
Special offers: This can include Buy One Get One Free (BOGOF) and other short-term promotions on selected items.	This can encourage customers to try new products, which they may then purchase again at normal price.	Customers might feel pressured into buying more than they need, which may result in waste.

Free gifts:		
Used to tempt customers to buy a product again or for the first time, e.g. a free toy in children's cereal.	Gifts that require multiple tokens/stamps can encourage repeat purchases.	It can be difficult to find a gift that appeals to all target markets, e.g. a free toy that suits boys and girls.
Vouchers and coupons:		
Usually given in newspapers/magazines to give customers money off future purchases.	Customers feel they are getting better value for money, which attracts new customers. It can encourage repeat purchases.	Discounts offered by money-off vouchers can reduce profits. Some customers will only spend up to the value of the money-off voucher, limiting sales.
Loyalty schemes:		
Allow customers to collect points by making purchases, which can then be exchanged for discounts or free products in the future, e.g. Tesco Clubcard.	Information on customer habits and preferences can be gathered. Promotions can be targeted to reflect actual customer preferences.	Customers can be wary if they feel the scheme will be difficult to set up or opt out of. These are time consuming and expensive to implement.
Interest-free credit:		
Retailers offer customers credit to pay for goods at a later date.	Allows customers to purchase products and then pay for them when they can afford to.	This could lead to bad debt if many customers are unable to pay by the agreed date.

Social media

Social media sites such as Facebook and Twitter are being used increasingly by businesses as a BTL promotion method.

Table 6.23 Advantages and disadvantages of social media as a BLT promotion method

Advantages	Disadvantages
The target market can be contacted directly, as they have 'liked' or 'followed' the business' social media page. This saves marketing to uninterested consumers.	It can be difficult to engage with new customers as they have to voluntarily agree to see the business' updates.
Information on new products or promotional offers, price changes or new products can be uploaded immediately.	It requires a lot of time to use social media effectively; larger businesses will have to employ someone to engage with social media full time.
The business can analyse those that like or follow them to find out their location/age/gender, which can allow them to target others effectively.	Negative feedback can be given, which can put other customers off using the business.
Consumers can leave comments which can be used to improve the product.	Negative feedback can be given instantly, not allowing the business time to release a statement in their defence.
Social media is free to use.	

Apps

Many businesses are now using **apps** designed for tablet computers and smartphones to promote their business. For example, Apple recently bought Beats in a $3 billion **takeover** (see page 12) primarily to acquire their *Music* app.

Table 6.24 Advantages and disadvantages of using apps for promotional purposes

Advantages	Disadvantages
Apps can target promotions and information on products that users will like, based on their browsing history.	Apps require a mobile signal to be used, limiting the reach to customers in rural locations.
Users of apps can share their experiences on social media sites, allowing the business free promotion and wider recognition.	There is a limit to the amount of information that can be put on apps due to the screen size of mobile devices.
Apps can have integrated services, such as airlines' online check-in services or online banking apps which increase usability.	Apps cost money to develop and are often given away for free.
E-commerce, (known as m-commerce on mobile devices) can be integrated, increasing sales potential to worldwide, 24/7.	Most apps, especially 'fun' apps that aim to promote businesses in a subliminal way, e.g. Nike's World Cup game app, have a very short shelf-life.
Information about products and offers can be updated quickly, keeping customers informed thus giving the organisation a good channel of communication.	Some customers are very uncertain about making purchases using M-commerce due to less secure virus protection than computers.
The app can integrate games, videos and photographs to grab users' attention and promote the business in a fun and engaging way.	

Product endorsement

Product endorsement involves businesses using celebrities (also known as **celebrity endorsement**) to promote the product. For example, Adidas pay Lionel Messi to wear their football boots and appear in their adverts.

Table 6.25 Advantages and disadvantages of product endorsements

Advantages	Disadvantages
The use of a celebrity will make consumers who like the celebrity more likely to purchase the product to be like them.	Some consumers will be put off a product if they don't like the celebrity that has been chosen to endorse it.
The product will be advertised for free every time the celebrity is spotted wearing or using it in public.	If a celebrity gains bad publicity it will tarnish the image of the products they are associated with.
If a celebrity gets good media coverage (e.g. winning a sports event), it will provide positive exposure for the product they are associated with.	It can be very expensive to pay celebrities to endorse products.
Higher prices can be charged as the use of a celebrity gives the product exclusivity.	Poor performance by celebrities (e.g. a sports star losing a sports event or an actor appearing in a box office flop), will result in lower sales of the products they endorse.
Brand loyalty can be created for as long as the celebrity is involved in the endorsement.	

Product placement

Product placement involves businesses paying for products to appear in films, TV shows or video games, for example, the brand of juice characters drink, the clothing brands they wear or the make of car they drive.

Table 6.26 Advantages and disadvantages of product placement

Advantages	Disadvantages
Awareness of products is generated, often to worldwide audiences.	The time of exposure can be very short, limiting the chances of consumers remembering the product they have seen.
It is a form of subliminal advertising – the audience doesn't know they are watching a promotion, they just watch the film.	Often, as a result of bidding wars with rival brands to secure the rights to appear in films, TV shows and games, product placement can cost a lot of money.
Products that can be identified with characters who customers like, can result in sales, as they want to be like the character or the actor who plays them.	Consumers may be put off certain products if they are associated with characters they don't like.
Merchandise 'spin-offs' can be sold, increasing sales on the back of a successful placement, e.g. the Wilson 'Hand' Volleyball from *Castaway*.	Products can appear as part of a negative storyline which can put customers off.

Case study 6.3

Back to the Future

In 1985, the science fiction film *Back to the Future* was the first film to use product placement on a large scale. The Irish sports car, Delorean featured prominently as the 'time machine' in the movie. Many other brands appear in the movie, such as Pepsi, Kellogg's and Pizza Hut, either as main props used by characters or just appearing in the background. The main character, Marty McFly even wore futuristic 'power laces' Nike trainers in the fictional future year of 2015, which Nike have now produced for real!

If you ever watch the film (or the entire trilogy!) be sure to watch out for the product placement.

Discussion points

In pairs, groups or on your own:

1 Explain why products being used by characters in TV and film is a good method of promotion.
2 Suggest the advantages of using products in a film about time travel.
3 Explain reasons why Nike produced the fictional trainers for real, to be launched in 2015.
4 Suggest other well-known products used in films you have seen.

Public relations

Public relations (PR) is the act of controlling the image of a business that is perceived by the public. Some larger businesses have their own dedicated PR Department. Table 6.27 shows methods used by PR to improve the image of an organisation.

Table 6.27 PR methods and justifications for using them

Method	Justification
Press conferences: The media are invited to a business presentation, where they are given information or news. A new or updated product might be launched.	Businesses can send a message or update out to a wide audience while keeping control, to a certain extent, of what is reported. It can help to get the media 'on side' and allows the press the opportunity to ask questions to the business directly.
Press releases: The media are provided with a written account of a business' newsworthy activities or events. Updated **mission statements** may also be released to the media.	This can be used to counteract bad publicity. Businesses can send out messages or updates without being subject to further questioning.
Donations to charities: Some businesses donate to charities anonymously, while others will take the opportunity for a good public relations event.	Promotes the CSR aims of the business and can make them seem ethical (see page 10). This can help the business achieve a positive image.
Sponsorship: Some businesses will pay to sponsor an event, team or venue. This is popular in the sporting industry.	Businesses can benefit from the successes of those that they sponsor. This can help businesses to become popular with customers who visit/support the sponsored event, team or venue.
Company visits: Businesses may choose to open up their factories to the public for a limited period.	Customers are able to get a sense of what the business is like and how it is run. The company may seem more friendly, approachable and open.

Factors affecting methods of promotion

The following factors can affect the promotion method chosen.

- **The target market** – Businesses should promote their products in places where they are likely to be seen by the target market. Market research feedback will help with this.
- **The finance available** – Every business would love to advertise at half time during the World Cup final but only the biggest marketing budgets will stretch to this. BTL methods are often used by smaller businesses for this reason.
- **The marketing mix** – All elements of the marketing mix should work in **synergy**. This means the methods are more effective when combined even though they work well as stand-alone elements. For example, the promotion of a model of GHD hair straighteners near the end of their life cycle (product) should be advertised in fashion magazines (promotion) informing the target market of a reduction in price if they buy them online (place).
- **Ethical practices** – Promotions should be **ethical** in order to avoid upsetting others. For example, promotions should not:
  - mislead customers
  - be indecent
  - make false claims designed to harm the competition.

The **Advertising Standards Agency** (ASA) is the governing body of all kinds of promotions. They ensure promotions are ethical, honest and decent, for example by regulating that products advertised as 'environmentally friendly' are in fact so.

Check out the work of the ASA for yourself at: **www.ASA.org.uk**

People

These final three 'P's are geared towards the marketing of the service customers receive. This is especially important for businesses operating in the tertiary sector, such as hotels, restaurants and banks; however, all businesses will have to provide services to customers at some point.

People refers to *who* is representing a business or a brand. Those employed by the business are essential to the image and reputation of a business, especially those that are **customer facing**, such as customer service assistants, receptionists and sales staff. The following steps should ensure the 'people' element of the marketing mix is successful:

Table 6.28 The 'people' element of the marketing mix

Method	Justification
Train staff well to deal with customers effectively.	This enables staff to be informed of the expectations of the business when dealing with customers, such as being polite and helpful.
Regularly update staff on product/service developments.	This ensures staff appear knowledgeable and can assist customers.
Ensure selection methods (see Chapter 4) are rigorous and staff aren't appointed on a 'whim'.	This ensures the people employed are suitable to represent the business and its values.
Monitor staff, e.g. by recording customer-service calls or sending mystery shoppers.	This ensures employees are representing the business appropriately and standards are maintained.

Process

Process refers to *how* a customer receives a service. This could be the *process* they go through to book a holiday, obtain a bank loan or even just select and pay for goods in a shop. The following steps should ensure the 'process' element of the marketing mix is successful:

Table 6.29 The 'process' element of the marketing mix

Method	Justification
Ensure that outlets and call centres are well staffed.	This avoids customers having to queue for too long, which can put them off returning.
Offer 'live chat' or 'FAQ' services on the business' website.	This reduces the number of customers making queries either on the phone or in person.
Empower customer-facing staff to make decisions.	This avoids further waiting as problems or queries do not need to be passed onto management.
Regularly assess processes such as queues or ordering times.	This helps the business understand where problems lie and allows them to be addressed.
Introduce the latest technologies to improve processes.	Technology is generally faster than humans and will speed up processes, e.g. self-checkouts in supermarkets.

Physical evidence

Physical evidence refers to *what* customers see that gives them clues about a business from the image it portrays. The following steps should ensure the 'physical evidence' element of the marketing mix is successful:

Table 6.30 The 'physical evidence' element of the marketing mix

Method	Justification
Premises and vehicles that are modern and clean.	This ensures that customers' opinion of the business isn't ruined by old-fashioned or dirty shops, reception areas or delivery vans.
Settings should convey the type of ambiance to match the product or service on offer.	This ensures that customers feel that their needs are recognised even before they purchase a good or service, e.g. the stylish and relaxing setting of an upmarket hair salon compared to the fun and colourful setting of a theme park.
Feedback and testimonials from previous customers should be promoted.	This provides reference materials for new customers which is especially important when purchasing a service as it can't be tried beforehand.

Case study 6.4
HSBC

HSBC has launched a fresh design concept for their branches to better meet the changing needs of its customers.

The new, open layout has sleek, modern furnishings in the bank's minimalist corporate colours of red, black and white. Inside there is sophisticated banking technology, areas for personal finance, as well as 'smart deposit' machines and 'express banking' terminals. The new branches also feature computers for customers to use internet banking services.

As part of the look and feel, most customer service staff have been taken out from behind the bullet-proof glass so they can speak to customers in private interview booths and consultation areas. A dedicated staff member even offers a friendly welcome at the entrance to the bank. $\Rightarrow$

⇒
Discussion points

In pairs, groups or on your own:

1 Identify elements of *people* that HSBC use to improve their marketing mix.
2 Identify elements of *process* that HSBC use to improve their marketing mix.
3 Identify elements of *physical evidence* that HSBC use to improve their marketing mix.
4 Explain reasons why HSBC's approach will attract customers.

Key questions 6.2

1 Describe the following marketing terms:
   a) product endorsement
   b) product placement.
2 Outline two into-the-pipeline promotions.
3 Describe two methods of direct selling.
4 Outline three extension strategies that could be used to extend a product's life.
5 Describe three methods a PR department could use to improve a business' image.
6 Describe the following pricing strategies:
   a) cost plus pricing
   b) price discrimination.
7 Describe three methods of distribution.
8 Suggest two ways a business could ensure their marketing activities are ethical.

Essential questions 6.2

1 **Explain** how two elements of the marketing mix can be improved to enhance the effectiveness of a large organisation.
2 **Describe** two advantages and two disadvantages of having a varied product portfolio.

Use of technology in marketing

Evidence of the use of technology in marketing has been abundant throughout this chapter. However, here is a summary of how technology can be used in the marketing function.

- The internet can be used to obtain market information from surveys or competitors' websites.
- The internet can also be used to advertise products, targeted through browsing histories.
- E-commerce can be used to sell products online.
- Social media can be used to interact with customers.
- Databases can be used to keep customer records and can be easily searched and merged into direct mail shots.

- Apps can be used to engage with customers, promote or sell products.
- SMS texts can be sent alerting customers of promotions.
- EPOS can be used to gain market research information.
- Self-checkout systems can be used to speed up the process of purchasing products.
- Digital screens can be used to display eye-catching advertisements.
- 3D can be used in cinemas and on TV to capture customers' attention during advertisements.

Key questions 6.3

1 Describe two benefits of using digital screens rather than traditional billboards to advertise products.
2 Suggest three ways in which smart-phones can be used in marketing activities.

Essential question 6.3

Describe how two types of technology are used in the marketing function.

Exam-style questions practice – Chapter 6

1 Explain the advantages and disadvantages of desk research as a source of market research information. **(4 marks)**
2 Describe factors affecting the pricing strategy a business chooses. **(5 marks)**
3 Describe the trends in retailer types in recent years. **(3 marks)**
4 Discuss the advantages and disadvantages of a retailer using a wholesaler rather than going to the manufacturer. **(5 marks)**
5 Explain the effect on profits and sales during the following stages of the product life cycle:
   a) development
   b) growth
   c) saturation. **(6 marks)**
6 Compare the following:
   a) market led and product led
   b) above-the-line promotions and below-the-line promotions.
      (4 marks)
7 Discuss the use of social media and mobile apps for interacting with customers. **(6 marks)**
8 Explain the benefits to a business of using e-commerce. **(4 marks)**

Chapter 7

Outcome 3.2: Management of Operations

What you should know

There are four main parts to this outcome. By the end of this outcome you should be able to:

1 **Describe** the features and purposes of inventory management systems.
2 **Explain** the benefits of methods that ensure quality products.
3 **Explain** the costs and benefits of production methods used by large organisations.
4 **Describe** how current technologies are used in the operations function.

Management of operations

It is the role of the operations department to provide the products that the organisation offers. Secondary sector organisations will be concerned with actually producing goods from raw materials, whereas tertiary sector will be concerned with the purchasing and stocking of goods or the systems that are in place to provide services to customers.

Inventory management

Inventory (stock) management is concerned with the sourcing and storage of raw materials (for secondary sector businesses) or supplies of finished goods for resale (for tertiary sector businesses).

Overstocking and understocking

Once a supplier is chosen, the business must then consider the quantity of stock to be ordered. A business must not overstock or understock as both have negative consequences.

Table 7.1 The consequences of overstocking and understocking

Consequences of overstocking	Consequences of understocking
Supplies could go out of date if they are stored for too long.	The business may run out of stock and be unable to continue production or carry on selling.
Supplies could go out of fashion before they are used.	The business will not benefit from bulk buying discounts due to making smaller orders.
Too many supplies leaves a risk of theft by staff, customers or thieves.	There may be no stock to sell, resulting in a bad reputation and customers not returning.
The business will have to pay for stockholding costs, such as insurance and security.	There will be an increase in delivery costs since many smaller deliveries will have to be made.
The **opportunity cost** of money being tied up in stock which could be better used elsewhere in the business.	There will be an increase in administration costs, e.g. paying staff to browse for supplies, complete order forms, settle invoices, etc.

Hints & tips

Although the consequences of over- and understocking are assessed at N5 level they can be used to answer questions across many topics in this chapter.

Inventory management systems

The following diagram illustrates the features of an inventory (stock) management system.

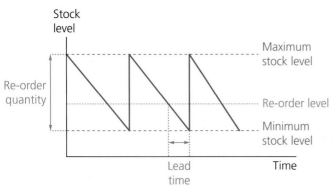

Figure 7.1 Features of an inventory management system.

As you can see from the diagram, the diagonal line illustrates inventory (stock) being used over time until it reaches the minimum level. Before the minimum level is reached a re-order level is triggered, allowing stock to be ordered once the minimum is reached. The vertical line illustrates the inventory (stock) level reaching the maximum again. The following table describes the features in more detail.

Table 7.2 Features of an inventory management system

Feature	Description	Justification
Maximum stock level	This is the most amount of inventory (stock) that should be held.	Setting this level avoids consequences of overstocking.
Minimum stock level	This is the least amount of inventory (stock) that should be held.	Setting this level avoids consequences of understocking.
Re-order level	The level at which stock is re-ordered. Computerised inventory systems link to EPOS and automatically re-order goods.	This avoids running out of stock.
Re-order quantity	This is the amount that is ordered.	This ensures the quantity ordered is not too much or too little.
Lead time	This is the time taken between an order being placed and stock arriving.	As short a lead time as possible allows the business to react to rush orders.

Setting inventory levels

The inventory management system is a guide. Each business will have to set their own specific levels, depending on the following factors:

- The **maximum stock level** depends on the storage available, the cost of storing goods and the maximum amount of demand.
- The **minimum stock level** depends on the relationship with suppliers, the skill levels of staff so materials are not wasted, the finance available, the minimum amount of demand and the likelihood of drastic changes to tastes and fashions.

- The **re-order level** depends on lead time, the amount of stock already held, if bulk-buying discounts are available, and the maximum and minimum stock levels themselves (see above).

Computerised stock control

Most inventory systems are now computerised. The advantages of this outweigh the disadvantages as seen in Table 7.3.

Table 7.3 Advantages and disadvantages of computerised stock control

Advantages	Disadvantages
Databases keep balances of inventory which are automatically updated.	Computerised systems will cost a lot of money to install and maintain.
Can be linked to tills through EPOS, which update inventory levels with each sale.	Money and time need to be invested to train staff to operate the system efficiently.
Accurate and constant monitoring of stock levels allows for automatic re-ordering.	
Allows for decisions on slow-moving stock or best sellers to be made by managers from their computers.	
Can highlight regional variations in stock for head office.	
Can highlight seasonal shifts in demand.	
Is a deterrent to theft by staff as they know inventory levels are monitored closely.	

Just in time

Just in time (JIT) is an alternative approach to inventory (stock) management. JIT is the process of ordering supplies only when they are either required for production or when an order is placed by a customer. JIT originated in Japan, a country renowned for 'lean' production techniques that increase efficiency and reduce wastage.

Table 7.4 Advantages and disadvantages of JIT

Advantages	Disadvantages
Allows production to be lean, i.e. there is no wastage as all stock is used for production.	If deliveries are late then the business will face the negative consequences of understocking.
No money is tied up in stock, improving cash flow and working capital.	Requires excellent relationships with suppliers to work effectively, which can take time to develop.
No warehouse is required, saving costs.	Relies on a good infrastructure between the business and suppliers, e.g. roads.
The business is more responsive to changing external factors.	No room for error in production.

> **Hints & tips** ★
>
> *The advantages and disadvantages of JIT are similar to those of understocking!*

Storage and warehousing

A business has to decide how to store its inventory (stock). Inventory is usually stored in **warehouses**. Large buildings in central locations are used to store inventory and distribute raw materials to factories or finished goods to retail outlets (called **centralised storage**). Warehouses can also be smaller buildings or areas of a factory or retail outlet (called **decentralised storage**).

Centralised storage

This involves storing inventory in one central location in a large, purpose-built **warehouse**.

Centralised storage has the following advantages and disadvantages.

Table 7.5 Advantages and disadvantages of centralised storage

Advantages	Disadvantages
Specialist staff are employed to maintain inventory, which improves speed of stock handling and security.	Inventory has to be delivered to the each division or department, causing delays.
Centralised warehouses can store a massive amount of stock, benefiting from economies of scale.	Specialist staff need to be employed to maintain inventory, increasing wage costs.
The same procedures for issuing inventory are used across the organisation, improving consistency.	Specialist equipment needs to be purchased and maintained.
It may be cheaper to store inventory in one large warehouse than the total cost of many smaller on-site storerooms.	Inventory usage levels and needs are unclear as divisions need to communicate with the warehouse.
Centralised warehouses are often located close to infrastructure, e.g. motorway networks, docks or air and rail cargo terminals.	The use of centralised warehousing has declined due to more efficient inventory systems such as JIT, sourcing direct from the supplier.

Decentralised storage

This involves storing inventory in many locations in smaller warehouses or store rooms.

Decentralised storage has the following advantages and disadvantages.

Table 7.6 Advantages and disadvantages of decentralised storage

Advantages	Disadvantages
Inventory is always close at hand when needed for production or to sell to customers.	Can lead to wastage or theft of stock as security isn't as good as it is in centralised storage.
Smaller, more local warehouses are more responsive to local needs.	Lack of specialist staff can lead to inventory control being clumsy and inefficient.
Inventory usage reflects production as it is stored in factories or retail outlets.	Each division may handle inventory differently, leading to inconsistency and problems being harder to pinpoint for senior management.
Smaller amounts of inventory result in no negative consequences of overstocking.	Smaller amounts of inventory result in negative consequences of understocking.

Hints & tips

Don't get centralised and decentralised storage confused with centralised and decentralised structures (see Chapter 1).

Case study 7.1

Amazon

Internet e-tailer Amazon couldn't possibly have a store of inventory in every town. Their approach is to have massive centralised warehouses that cater for entire sections of the country. The picture above is of the biggest warehouse in the UK, located near Dunfermline in Fife. It is the size of 14 football pitches! The site is located next to the M90 and A92, so it is within easy reach of Edinburgh, Stirling and St Andrews, as well as towns and cities to the north, south and west.

Warehouse staff receive, pack and ship items for Amazon customers every day. A central computer records the location of goods and maps out routes for warehouse staff. Staff carry hand-held computer devices which communicate with the central computer and monitor their rate of progress.

Discussion points

In pairs, groups or on your own:

1 Suggest reasons why Amazon's Fife warehouse is a good example of centralised storage.
2 Describe the advantages of the location of Amazon's Fife warehouse.
3 Explain the use of technology at Amazon's Fife warehouse.

Logistics management

In large organisations, **logistics managers** are responsible for inventory, storage and distribution. Firstly, logistics managers need to have an understanding of **channels of distribution** (see page 101). They also need to understand the network of suppliers that provide materials for production (known as the **supply chain**), so they can co-ordinate effectively and liaise with suppliers of raw materials, manufacturers, retailers and consumers.

Technology also plays a big part in the role, as automated systems and electronic communication methods are used to keep track of inventory levels, delivery times, transport costs and performance evaluation. Logistics managers must also be aware of external factors that can affect **methods of distribution** (see page 20) such as:

Figure 7.2 Logistics is now utilising low emissions trucks to be environmentally friendly and to lower fuel costs.

- **Legislation**: for example, the amount of time drivers can work without rest will increase delivery times unless arrangements are made, perhaps for 'substitute' drivers.
- **Fuel costs**: rises will impact on profits unless they are passed onto customers.
- **Environmental pressures**: trying to reduce carbon footprint will mean environmentally friendly methods of distribution need to be considered, such as low-emissions trucks.

The role of the logistics manager

Let's look again at the role of a manager (see page 46) to understand exactly what logistic managers do:

1 *Planning* inventory required using **production** and **sales budgets**
2 *Organising* for the resources needed for logistics, including **warehouse** equipment and staff

3 *Commanding* warehouse staff to carry out tasks
4 *Co-ordinating* the supply chain, channels and methods of distribution so deliveries are made on time
5 *Controlling* the quality, quantity, cost and efficiency of the movement and storage of inventory, etc.
6 *Delegating* inventory procedures to **decentralised** warehouses
7 *Motivating* other members of their team.

Methods of distribution

Hints & tips

Don't get confused between channels of distribution and methods of (physical) distribution!

Table 7.7 Methods of distribution and their advantages and disadvantages

Method	Advantages	Disadvantages
Road: Products distributed via the road network.	Generally a quick and efficient method, especially for short journeys. Allows door-to-door delivery to and from any location, 24 hours a day. Refrigerated vehicles can be used to transport perishable products.	Delays on the roads and adverse weather can hold up deliveries. Can be expensive due to increasing fuel costs.
Rail: Products distributed via railways.	Some businesses have private rail lines linked to distribution centres. Useful for heavy goods. A more environmentally friendly method.	The rail terminal is generally not the final destination of the goods. This could incur road haulage costs. Not suitable in some areas, e.g. rural locations. Specialist rail-freight terminals are required.
Air: Products distributed via airmail, e.g. FedEx.	Ideal for long distances and more remote locations. Quick deliveries can be made overseas.	The airport is not the final destination. This could incur road haulage costs. Often a more expensive method than others.
Sea: Products distributed via shipping lanes.	Useful for importing or exporting heavy or bulky products.	The dock is not the final destination. This could incur road haulage costs. A slower method meaning longer delivery times.
Satellite: Services sent via satellite signal, e.g. TV or satnav.	Services can be distributed directly to the customer's location.	Signals can be disrupted due to adverse weather. High installation costs.
Utilities infrastructure: Services sent via underground or overhead lines, i.e. gas pipelines, electricity lines, fibre optic and cable TV.	Services can be distributed directly to the customer's location. Infrastructure is being improved every year, especially in busy areas.	Service can be disrupted due to adverse weather. High installation costs. Rural areas could be disadvantaged as it is prohibitively expensive to install the infrastructure in these areas.
Mobile networks: Service sent via wireless signals from mobile phone masts to customer devices.	Extra products can be purchased using the network, e.g. the increase in m-commerce (purchasing products via mobiles). 4G is now available which increases signal strength and access to the internet.	Signal can be disrupted due to adverse weather. Rural areas could be disadvantaged (see above).

Key questions 7.1

1 Discuss one advantage and one disadvantage of just in time (JIT) stock control.
2 Describe two features of logistics management.
3 Draw and label a stock control management system.

Essential questions 7.1

1 **Describe** two features of an inventory (stock) control management system.
2 **Explain** two purposes of an inventory (stock) control management system.

Production

Budgeting

Budgeting is not just used by the finance department. In fact, it is also used in operations and marketing.

Sales budgets

Sales budgets are firstly produced by the marketing department. Their purpose is to:
- provide targets for sales staff to aim for
- be used in conjunction with bonuses or commission for meeting targets
- motivate sales staff to reach targets.

Production budgets

Production budgets are created by using information from the sales budget. Their purpose is to:
- plan production so that there are enough goods to meet anticipated sales
- allow enough raw materials to be purchased so there is no understocking
- allow for not too many raw materials to be purchased so there is no overstocking.

Methods of production

Job production

Job production involves producing unique, one-off products. Products are made to order, one at a time from start to finish. Examples include large public spending projects such as the new Forth Bridge. Job production can also be for smaller-scale items made to a customer's specific requirements, such as a tailor-made suit or prom dress.

Table 7.8 Advantages and disadvantages of job production

Advantages	Disadvantages
Higher prices can be charged as the product is unique and made to customer requirements.	High wages need to be paid to the highly skilled staff that job production requires.
Products can match exact requirements, which increases customer satisfaction.	High costs can make the price too high, which can put many customers off.

The job can be altered once it has started to meet changing requirements.	Expensive tools and machinery may be required, which can often lie idle during different jobs.
Employees are more motivated as each project is slightly different and not mundane.	Lead times can be lengthy meaning customers cannot simply walk in and purchase the product.
The business can stay ahead of competitors by offering non-standard products.	Materials may need to be ordered for each individual job, missing out on bulk buying discounts.

Batch production

Batch production involves making groups of identical products at a time. Each batch is exactly the same, e.g. same flavour, colour or style. One batch is made, say of one flavour, then the machines that were used will be cleaned and another batch of another flavour will be made. Batch production is common in the food industry.

Table 7.9 Advantages and disadvantages of batch production

Advantages	Disadvantages
Batches can be adapted to meet customer requirements.	Equipment and staff often sit idle between batches as tooling and machines need to be cleaned and reset.
Batches can be adapted to take advantage of seasonal factors, e.g. flavours being adapted to tie in with summer events like a World Cup or the Olympics.	If a mistake is made it can ruin an entire batch, unlike job production whereby only one product is ruined.
Machinery can be standardised, which saves costs.	Employees are likely to be demotivated as tasks are repetitive.
There is less need for highly skilled workers.	Small batches can raise the unit cost of each item in the batch.
Materials can be bought in bulk, gaining discounts.	High stock levels are required, leading to the negative consequences of overstocking.

Flow production

Flow production involves identical products being made on an assembly line. The product is made in stages, with parts being added as it moves along the assembly line. Examples of flow production include the production of cars and computers.

Case study 7.2
Ford

When cars were first invented they were made to order (job production); however, very few cars were sold as they were so expensive. Henry Ford pioneered not only the first *car* assembly line, but the first assembly line to be used to make *any* consumer good in large quantities, known as **mass production**!

Figure 7.3 The Model T assembly line.

The 'Model T' Ford car was the first car to be mass produced. Each car would start off at one end of the assembly line as a basic frame and parts would be added, such as the wheels, engine and bodywork, as it passed on from one section to the next. Unlike modern assembly lines which are mostly **automated** (capital intensive), in 1908 most of the work was done by hand (labour intensive). Each worker would do the same job over and over again. This enabled him to become skilled and fast at doing the job; this is known as **specialisation**. There was one main drawback of the Model T, as Henry Ford said himself, 'You can have it in any colour you want, as long as it's black!'

$\Rightarrow$

Discussion points
In pairs, groups or on your own:

1 Suggest reasons why car production was so expensive before the Model T was invented.
2 Explain why assembly lines lower unit costs.
3 Discuss the differences between capital and labour intensive.
4 Explain what you think Henry Ford meant by his famous quote.

Table 7.10 Advantages and disadvantages of flow production

Advantages	Disadvantages
Huge amounts of products can be produced (mass production). This leads to very high sales.	Products cannot be adapted to meet customer requirements (see Henry Ford's quote).
Workers specialise in the same routine task, speeding up production and accuracy.	Workers can be demotivated through the boredom of doing the same routine tasks.
It is often capital intensive, e.g. robotics are used, which increases consistency, quality and the amount that can be produced.	If there is a fault in the production line then all production grinds to a halt, leaving staff and machines idle.
There are economies of scale from buying in bulk.	Massive amounts of investment are needed to equip and tool factories.

Capital-intensive production

Capital-intensive production involves producing products that primarily use machinery and equipment to produce products.

Capital-intensive production can utilise either **automation** or **mechanisation**.

Automation
Automation refers to production being fully *automatic*. This involves the use of **computer aided manufacture** (CAM) to control fully automated assembly lines that use **robotics** as seen in Figure 7.5. Compare this to the picture of the Model T Ford **labour-intensive** production line.

Figure 7.4 Fully automated, capital-intensive production, using robotics to manufacture cars.

Using automation has the following advantages and disadvantages:

Table 7.11 Advantages and disadvantages of automation

Advantages	Disadvantages
CAM/robotics produce products in exactly the same way every time, improving consistency.	Huge investment is needed to automate a production line.
CAM doesn't lose concentration so less mistakes are made, which limits waste.	Breakdowns can be catastrophic, losing hours of production time and wasting vast amounts of materials.
Robots can do jobs that are dangerous for humans to do.	Replacing labour with automated robotics will demotivate retained employees.
Robots don't take breaks, holidays or sick leave so can work 24/7.	Absence of a 'human touch', often leads to lack of creativity and personality in the products produced.
Fewer employees are needed as automation doesn't require human control, reducing wage costs.	

Mechanisation
Mechanisation refers to labour and machines working together to produce products. A traditional example is a machinist operating a sewing machine in a textile factory.

Table 7.12 Advantages and disadvantages of mechanisation

Advantages	Disadvantages
Using machinery improves accuracy over purely hand made products as human error is lessened.	The machines and equipment can't be used without humans, so are liable to some human error.
Using machinery can speed up production.	Production can't be 24/7 as humans require breaks, holidays, and so on.
Unlike automation, a human element exists in mechanisation, improving creativity.	If machinery breaks down the business has to repair it, leaving workers idle.

Labour-intensive production

Labour-intensive production involves humans doing *most* of the work. This is most common in **job production**, for example, skilled hand-crafts, such as cake decorating.

Labour-intensive production has the following advantages and disadvantages.

> **Hints & tips**
>
> Some **mechanisation** could be classed as labour intensive, depending on whether it is the machine or the human doing most of the work, for example, a joiner using power tools.

Table 7.13 Advantages and disadvantages of labour intensive production

Advantages	Disadvantages
Labour is less expensive than capital intensive production.	The business is at high risk of human error, resulting in waste, faulty products and disgruntled customers.
Humans can use initiative and creativity, something that is often lacking in automated systems.	Humans have to take breaks, holidays, etc., which limits production time.
There's a constant supply of labour, often skilled labour, available in areas of the country with manufacturing traditions.	Humans have to be paid overtime for working over normal hours whereas machines cost the same at any time of day.
Employees are motivated as they are not 'giving up' tasks to machines.	Recruitment, training and wage costs need to be considered.

Factors affecting method of production

The method of production chosen will depend on the following factors.

Table 7.14 Factors affecting method of production

Factor	Description
Quantity of goods required	If large quantities are required, flow or batch production will be more suitable than job production.
Skills of the workforce	If the workforce is highly skilled, their expertise would be better suited to job production.
Cost of labour	Rising labour costs (perhaps due to a rising minimum wage) could mean that the business should move to capital-intensive production.
Finance available	Large amounts of finance are required to equip factories or hire the number of staff needed for large-scale flow production.
Technology available	If the business doesn't have the technology required for capital-intensive production, labour intensive is the only option.

Key questions 7.2

1 Describe two purposes of a production budget.
2 Discuss one advantage and one disadvantage of labour-intensive production.
3 Describe the meaning of the term 'specialisation'.

Essential questions 7.2

1 **Describe** two production methods used by large organisations.
2 **Explain** one advantage and one disadvantage of the methods you
   described in essential question 1.

Quality

It is important for the operations department to ensure goods are of
good **quality** for the following reasons:

- Poor quality goods can result in customers returning their purchases,
  causing a loss in sales.
- Extremely low quality can result in products not meeting safety
  standards, which can lead to bad PR.
- Conversely, high-quality goods can result in a good reputation.
- Being associated with quality production can attract high-quality staff.
- The highest quality goods can be sold for premium prices.

Quality control

Quality control is the most basic method of ensuring quality. Quality
control is a method of **inspecting** raw materials or finished goods to
check they are of an acceptable standard and quality.

Table 7.15 Advantages and disadvantages of quality control

Advantages	Disadvantages
Ensures that faulty goods are not sent to customers.	Can create a lot of waste as the quality of the goods are not checked until they are made and have to be thrown away if they do not meet quality standards.
Limits the potential for a bad reputation due to faulty products.	Products have to be reworked from scratch, costing the business time and money.

Quality assurance

Quality assurance is a method of **prevention**, i.e. where products are
checked to see that they are of high quality at different stages in the
development and production process rather than just at the end.
For example, a **quality assurance manager** might check the raw
materials, inspect the machinery, speak to employees, sample work in
progress and inspect finished goods.

Table 7.16 Advantages and disadvantages of quality assurance

Advantages	Disadvantages
Less wastage, which decreases costs spent on discarded materials.	Can slow down production as many processes are inspected.
Easy to identify where faults in the production process lie.	Can increase the costs of production, e.g. paying QA managers' wages.

Quality improvement

Organisations should always attempt to improve quality, even if it has met its objectives. This is known as **quality improvement**. A Japanese philosophy known as **kaizen** should be considered by businesses looking to improve. Kaizen is the philosophy of everyone and every process in the organisation *continuously improving*.

Table 7.17 Advantages and disadvantages of quality improvement

Advantages	Disadvantages
The business stays ahead of the competition.	The business can have high staff-development costs.
The business can react easily to changing external factors.	Employees may feel under pressure to continually keep improving.

Quality circles

A **quality circle** is another Japanese philosophy on how to improve quality and ensure efficiency. They involve a group of employees meeting with a line manager to discuss problems in the production process and how to solve them. Suggestions are then passed to management for further discussion and may then be implemented.

Table 7.18 Advantages and disadvantages of quality circles

Advantages	Disadvantages
Employees will be motivated as they get to have a say in decision-making.	Employees meet during paid company time, meaning production time is lost.
Management get well-informed suggestions from the workers who actually produce the product.	Employees are often trained to join a quality circle, costing the business even more time and money.

Quality standards and symbols

A **quality standard** or **symbol** proves that a product has met an agreed industry standard. For example, hotels that meet standards to achieve a 'star' rating, such as a 5-star hotel. BSI, the business standards company is renowned for its marks of excellence including the globally recognised BSI Kitemark™.

WWW

Find out more about the BSI for yourself by logging on to:
www.bsigroup.com

Table 7.19 Advantages and disadvantages of quality standards and symbols

Advantages	Disadvantages
Awards prove to customers that a product has met an agreed standard of quality.	Time consuming processes need to be completed to achieve the award.
Symbols can be used as a promotional tool to gain a competitive edge.	Agreed standards need to be maintained at all times.
Customers will have confidence in purchasing the product and may repeat purchase.	If any award is removed it would give the organisation a poor reputation.
Higher prices can be charged as the product is of high quality.	Annual checks and audits by awarding bodies can disrupt production.

Case study 7.3

BSI Kitemark

Having a BSI Kitemark associated with a product or service confirms that it has been independently checked to prove that it conforms to a particular standard, and that it has also been checked consistently over time. It is one of the most recognised symbols of quality and safety and offers true value to consumers, businesses and procurement practices.

The BSI Kitemark originated as the British Standards Mark in 1903 for use on tramway rails when standardisation reduced the number of rail sizes from 75 to 5. The BSI Kitemark can be seen on hundreds of products from manhole covers to condoms, from security locks to fire extinguishers and riding helmets and includes service related schemes too such as the installation of windows and doors and the repair of vehicles after they have been in an accident. Today the newest BSI Kitemark schemes help consumers identify banking apps they can trust and, help banking customers quickly and easily identify financial products they can trust to meet their essential needs.

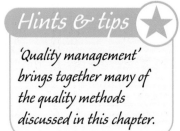

Figure 7.5 The BSI Kitemark is a sign of quality, safety and trust, reassuring customers that safety standards have been met.

Discussion points

Why is it important for:

1 businesses
2 consumers
3 procurement (buying) departments

for products to be awarded the BSI Kitemark.

Benchmarking

Benchmarking involves copying the quality of a finished product, and the processes used to achieve it, used by the market leader.

Table 7.20 Advantages and disadvantages of benchmarking

Advantages	Disadvantages
If successful, the product will be as good as the best on the market.	Can be difficult to gain information about other organisation's quality methods.
Saves the business time developing their own approach to ensuring quality.	The business will only ever be 'as good' as the benchmark at a time. The benchmark may improve, leaving the organisation behind. The business will never be better than the benchmark, so will never be market leader.

Quality management

Quality management is a *holistic* approach to ensuring quality products. This means it incorporates not just one method but takes into account a variety of methods, including quality assurance, quality improvement and quality circles. Quality management ensures *all people* in an organisation are committed to quality to ensure **zero errors** occur. Organisations that prove they carry out quality management can be awarded the ISO 9001 quality standard.

> **Hints & tips** ⭐
>
> *'Quality management' brings together many of the quality methods discussed in this chapter.*

Table 7.21 Advantages and disadvantages of quality management

Advantages	Disadvantages
Quality management should result in zero errors, which drastically reduces waste.	Substantial staff training, to ensure no mistakes are made, will increase costs and result in lost work time.
Staff are motivated, as they are constantly consulted on improving quality.	Requires the commitment of *all* staff, which could require a stricter selection process.
Products will be renowned for being of the highest quality, increasing customer confidence and market share.	Processes need to be continually monitored and compared to policies and procedures, which can be time consuming.
A culture of teamwork is established, as everyone works together to improve.	

Mystery shoppers

People are employed, often through an agency, to purchase products, ask questions, register complaints or behave in a certain way, and then provide feedback to the business about the experiences they had.

Table 7.22 Advantages and disadvantages of mystery shopping

Advantages	Disadvantages
The mystery shopper is not employed by or directly connected to the business. This means no bias is shown.	Staff may resent a mystery shopper evaluating them, if they are aware of it, and may take the feedback personally.
Valuable feedback, which may be lost when a customer chooses simply not to buy a product, is gathered when a product is below standard or unsatisfactory.	The mystery shopper's feedback may not be fully representative of the business as a whole as it provides a limited evaluation, i.e. one day, one branch, one customer service assistant, etc.
The mystery shopper can suggest improvements that ensure a better match between the experience that the customer *actually* has and the one the business *intends* them to have.	Allowances have to be made for human error in judgements. Mystery shoppers are people who have feelings and opinions, which may cloud their judgement from time to time.
Dissatisfied customers are likely to share their poor experiences with others, whereas the mystery shopper is *not permitted* to do this.	Businesses need to pay mystery shoppers, often through an agency, increasing costs.

Key questions 7.3

1. Suggest two reasons why organisations should ensure quality.
2. Describe three features of quality management.
3. Describe two advantages of using mystery shoppers as a method to ensure quality.

Essential questions 7.3

1. **Describe** two methods to ensure quality.
2. **Explain** two benefits of *each* method described in essential question 1.

Ethical and environmental issues

Operations, in conjunction with the marketing department, need to consider how their products impact on **ethics** and the **environment**. By ensuring both are considered, an organisation will ensure they meet the **CSR** objectives (see page 10).

Ethical issues

Organisations should try to be **ethical**. This means they show moral consideration for others when making decisions.

Table 7.23 Advantages and disadvantages of being ethical

Advantages	Disadvantages
Awards can be granted for being ethical, which can be used for promotional purposes.	Audits are needed to ensure standards are met and maintained, which may be time consuming.
Businesses with an ethical reputation can attract customers and quality staff who agree with their principles.	Decision-making could be more complex and time consuming as many possible solutions may not be appropriate because they are not ethical.

Philanthropy

Philanthropy means having a 'love for humanity'. In other words, giving to those in need. This could be through charitable donations, giving away goods or setting up a charitable trust as part of the organisation.

Animal welfare

The moral considerations of an organisation need not only refer to how people are treated, increasingly these concerns are also around the treatment and wellbeing of animals. This might include the conditions that animals are kept in, the way they are handled, animal testing and the use of animal-derived ingredients.

Examples of ways that organisations can prove their commitment to animal welfare include:

- The 'leaping bunny' symbol awarded to products that are entirely cruelty free.
- The free range classification of eggs and egg-derived products
- The use of synthetic materials rather than leather, fur or wool.

Figure 7.6 The 'leaping bunny' symbol is awarded to companies whose products are free from animal testing.

Fair trade

Fair trade is when suppliers of raw materials receive a guaranteed and fair price for their goods. Fair trade also ensures that employees in the supply chain are treated fairly.

Organisations are encouraged to use suppliers that are part of the Fairtrade Foundation.

Table 7.24 Advantages and disadvantages of fair trade

Advantages	Disadvantages
Businesses are awarded the Fairtrade mark on their products, which can appeal to customers.	Losing a Fairtrade mark after gaining one will result in bad publicity.
Stocking fair trade goods demonstrates the retailer's ethical commitment to its customers.	Fair trade products are often more expensive.
Businesses that are fair trade have a positive impact on the producers of the raw materials with which they work and have a better relationship with the supply chain.	The business has a more limited choice of suppliers.

Find out more about how businesses can get involved with fair trade: **www.fairtrade.org.uk/en/for-business**

Environmental issues

Organisations should do their bit to help the environment. This will have the following advantages and disadvantages.

Table 7.25 Advantages and disadvantages of being environmentally friendly

Advantages	Disadvantages
The organisation plays a part in looking after the environment that will hopefully sustain their activities for the future.	Investment in environmentally friendly measures will be expensive in the short-term, e.g. installing solar panels.
Having a positive effect on the environment will ensure the organisation gains a positive reputation.	New procedures may have to be adapted to be more environmentally friendly, which can take time.
Awards can be granted for being 'environmentally friendly', which can be used for promotional purposes.	Most environmentally friendly procedures rely on the natural environment, which may not be sufficient, e.g. lack of wind, solar energy, etc.
Renewable energies save costs in the long run as fuels such as oil, petrol or gas don't need to be paid for.	

Carbon footprint

This refers to the impact that using fossil fuels, such as oil and gas, has on the environment. Examples of ways that organisations can prove their commitment to reducing their carbon footprint are:

- using alternative sources of 'renewable' energy, such as solar and wind, for example to power premises.
- using low emissions vehicles or EVs (electric vehicles) for deliveries and company cars.
- using altogether more environmentally friendly **methods of distribution** can be used (see page 120).

Sustainable raw materials

Being **sustainable** refers to ensuring that the raw materials used by a business activity are not being depleted. As well as respecting the natural environment and gaining a good reputation, this will ensure that businesses can source raw materials in the future.

Examples of ways that organisations can prove their commitment to this are:

- **replanting** raw materials that are used in production, for example, Velvet toilet roll's commitment to replace three trees for every one that it uses
- **reusing** or **recycling** materials to be used in production
- **using resources responsibly**, for example, sustainable fishing limits the amount of fish that can be caught in an area to allow the fish to breed and naturally replenish
- **utilising renewable energies**.

Figure 7.7 Velvet commits to replacing three trees for each one it uses to produce toilet roll.

Waste

Not only does committing to dealing with **waste** appropriately help the environment, it is a *legal responsibility* to store, transport and dispose of waste without harming the environment.

Organisations must ensure they comply with the following, **duty of care** when dealing with waste:

- **segregate** waste appropriately, for example, keeping apart chemicals that may react
- **store** waste appropriately, for example, securing waste
- **transport** waste appropriately and securely.

Packaging

As well as being part of **below-the-line** promotion, the packaging of products should be designed to be as environmentally friendly as possible. The 'green' qualities of packaging can even be promoted to help the product gain a good image.

Ways that packaging could be environmentally friendly include:
- being **reusable**. This means the packaging can be used again in its current format, for example, 'bags for life' or Barr's glass bottles being re-filled and sold again.
- being **recyclable**. This means the packaging can be recycled easily into something else, saving the use of fresh raw materials, for example, Lush recycle their plastic containers into scarves.
- being **biodegradable**. This means used packaging can break down more easily. The least biodegradable packaging is hard plastic bottle caps which can take up to 400 years to decompose!

Case study 7.4

SEPA

The **Scottish Environmental Protection Agency** (SEPA) is a public sector organisation that helps businesses improve their environmental responsibilities. SEPA offer guidelines on the following environmental responsibilities in a document available on their website:

- **land contamination** (e.g. accidental spills of solvents and oils)
- **noise and odour pollution** (e.g. vehicle movement, waste handling, storage and transportation)
- **energy usage** (e.g. poorly maintained machinery, inefficient procedures and motors)
- **waste disposal** (e.g. such as solid and liquid wastes – must comply with **duty of care**)

SEPA suggest that businesses that follow their guidelines will reap the following benefits:

- improving **efficiency** and **productivity** by building a **sustainable** business
- reducing **waste** and associated **expenses**
- improving **reputation** amongst staff, customers, suppliers and the public
- increasing the chance of **funding** by demonstrating environmental responsibility
- improving **legal compliance**, less chance of **prosecution**, and fewer time-consuming visits from environmental regulators.

Discussion points

In pairs, groups or on your own:

1 Suggest ways businesses could comply with the main environmental responsibilities outlined by SEPA.
2 Explain the benefits to a business of following SEPA guidelines.
3 Explain the costs to a business of not taking SEPA guidelines on board.

www 🖱

Find out more about what SEPA do for yourself by logging on to:
www.sepa.org.uk

Use of technology in operations

Here is a summary of how technology can be used in the operations function.

- IT, for example laptops/tablets/smartphones and email, can be used to purchase supplies quickly.
- The internet can be used to research supplier prices.
- EPOS can be used with computerised stock control to automatically reorder depleted stock.
- Computerised devises can be used by warehouse staff to check and find stock.
- Automated systems can track deliveries for both the business' and the customer's information.
- Spreadsheets can be used to accurately and quickly produce production budgets.
- CAM (computer aided manufacture), such as robotics, can be used in automated production.
- Emerging technologies such as solar energy, wind energy and EV can be used to harness renewable energy.

Activity 7.1 ✏

Now that we have covered all the functional areas, you may have noticed that there is some crossover when it comes to the technology used.

A useful revision activity is to look at the main software and technology, and summarise how it is used in each function.

	Technology					
	Spreadsheet	Word processing	Databases	E-mail	Video-conferencing	Internet
Human Resources						
Finance						
Marketing						
Operations						

1. Copy the above table, either on paper or using a word-processing package.
2. Try and write down a use of each piece of technology, specific for each functional department.
3. Ask your teacher or lecturer to check your work, but don't worry if you can't get all uses for all functions; we haven't covered all possibilities in this book.

Key questions 7.4

1 Discuss one advantage and one disadvantage of using Fairtrade certified suppliers.
2 Describe two ways technology can enable businesses to be more environmentally friendly.

Essential question 7.4

Describe how two types of technology are used in the operations function.

Exam-style questions practice – Chapter 7

1 Describe factors that affect the method of production chosen by a business. **(4 marks)**
2 Compare the following:
   a) capital intensive and labour intensive
   b) mechanisation and automation. **(4 marks)**
3 Explain factors that will be considered when setting a minimum stock level. **(3 marks)**
4 Discuss the advantages and disadvantages of quality circles. **(5 marks)**
5 Describe the advantages to a large multinational of using centralised warehouses to store materials. **(4 marks)**
6 Explain the ways an operation department can achieve the ethical and environmental considerations of a positive corporate social responsibility (CSR) policy. **(5 marks)**

Answers and solutions

Key questions 1.1

1 Private sector: businesses owned by private individuals.

Public sector: organisations owned by the government.

Third sector: organisations that aim to aid others.

2 Primary sector: raw materials are extracted from their natural environment.
Secondary sector: raw materials are turned into goods.

Tertiary sector: services are provided to consumers, such as selling goods.

Quaternary sector: consists of providing information and knowledge-based services, such as R&D.

3 PLCs are owned by shareholders.

Shares in a PLC can be sold publicly on the stock market.

Shareholders in PLCs have limited liability, i.e. they can only lose their investment and not personal possessions to creditors.

4 Two third-sector organisations are:
- Charities which exist to raise money to help others, for example, Cancer Research.
- Social enterprises, which are businesses that aim to maximise profits to help a particular cause, e.g. the Big Issue helps the homeless.

Essential question 1.1

- A PLC is owned by shareholders *whereas* a public sector organisation is owned by the government.
- A PLC is financed through selling shares on the stock market *whereas* a public sector organisation is financed through taxes collected from the general public.

Key questions 1.2

1 Corporate social responsibility refers to organisations aiming to act in a way that benefits either society or the environment.
2 a) A merger is when two businesses agree to become one organisation.
   b) A de-merger is when an organisation splits into two separate organisations.
   c) Divestment is selling off part of a business.
3 Businesses will be able to take advantage of economies of scale, such as bulk buying.

Businesses will be able to spread risk over more products/outlets, etc.

Business will lessen the chance of being taken over.

Essential questions 1.2

1 Maximise profits

Corporate social responsibility
2 A PLC would want to maximise profits so they have as much money as possible to pay shareholders' dividends and invest in the business.

A PLC would want to have CSR aims so they build a good reputation among society and gain more customers.

Answers

Key questions 1.3

1 The chain of command is the flow of information and decisions through an organisation.

2 Advantages:
- Each team has specialised staff from all functional areas.
- A matrix structure can be motivational for staff.

Disadvantages:
- High wage costs.
- Staff can be confused about who to report to.

3 A tall management structure has many levels of management *whereas* a flat management structure has few levels of management.

Essential questions 1.3

1 An organisation could use functional groupings. This is when common areas of expertise and skills are grouped together, such as a marketing department, a finance department, etc.

An organisation could use an entrepreneurial management structure. This is when the business has very few key decision-makers at the core of the organisation, usually only the owner.

2 An organisation would use a functional grouping as everyone is clear about their roles and responsibilities, giving the organisation a clear structure and staff know who to turn to for advice

A business could use an entrepreneurial structure as they have few decision-makers so decisions can be made quickly.

Answers

Key questions 2.1

1 Managers can impact on an organisation by the level of risk they are willing to take or by the experience they have.

Employees can impact on an organisation through the level of training and skill they have and the levels of motivation they have to do a good job.

2 Robotics could be used in production to produce goods with consistency, at a high volume output, 24/7.

E-commerce could be used to sell online to a global market, 24/7.

Apps could be used to give businesses a presence on mobile technology, such as smartphones and tablets, and keep businesses up to date by interacting with customers.

3 Corporate culture is the set of values, beliefs and customs that is shared by all people in an organisation.

4 Uphold company values, such as a commitment to recycling or fair trade.

Adopt corporate colours, such as Easy Jet's orange or Coca Cola's red.

Have an open and relaxed office layout.

Introduce flexible working arrangements, such as homeworking or flexitime, which allow employees to work when and where suits them best.

Essential question 2.1

Employees could affect the organisation by not being motivated, which means the standard of their work might drop, or they may provide poor customer service, which could lead to customer complaints.

The finance available could affect the organisation as if there is no money it will not be able to carry out decisions and courses of action it wishes to, such as expanding the business.

Key questions 2.2

1 Income tax

VAT

Corporation tax

2 Fiscal policy is when the government controls spending through tax changes and public spending on infrastructure and large projects *whereas* monetary policy is when the Bank of England controls the supply of the public's money by changing interest rates.

3 Social:
- UK's ageing population has seen a growth in products and services for the elderly.
- There has been a rise in women taking up professional careers and managerial positions.

Technological:
- Cloud computing has enabled organisations to store and access information remotely.
- Social networking has enabled organisations to keep constant communication with customers on sites like Facebook.

4 Positive: Competition could open up a store next to a business, which brings more passing trade to the area.

Negative: Competition could offer lower prices or better quality products, which would attract customers away.

Essential question 2.2

Political factors could impact on a large organisation. The government could increase the minimum wage. This would mean the organisation had to pay more wages which would result in a smaller profit.

Economic factors could impact on a large organisation. The economy could be in a recession. This would mean there is high unemployment which results in customers having less money to spend in the organisation, reducing sales.

Key questions 2.3

1 A stakeholder is an individual or group of people who have an interest in the success of an organisation.
2 The Inland Revenue want to ensure businesses and employees are paying the correct taxes.
3 Customers can decide not to buy from the business and go to the competition.
4 Owners need governments to make good decisions, such as lowering taxes to improve the spending power of customers, *while* governments need owners to create jobs in the community.

Essential question 2.3

Employees want a pay rise *whereas* owners want to keep wages low to maximise profits.

Customers want low prices and value for money *whereas* owners want to raise prices to maximise profits.

Answers

Key questions 4.1

1 Recruitment is the process of getting employees to apply for a job, for example, advertising the job, *whereas* selection is the process of choosing from the applicants by narrowing them down, for example, through testing.

2 New staff may be needed, for example due to increasing demand for existing products. Existing staff may have to be removed due to retirement, maternity leave, etc.

3 Step 1 – The organisation analyses the potential demand for its goods/services and decides how many staff are needed and the skills required.

   Step 2 – The organisation analyses the profile of its current workforce to determine the need for new staff or the development training needs of existing staff.

   Step 3 – The organisation 'closes the gaps' to ensure that it has the workforce required to provide the goods and services to meet its objectives, e.g. by training existing staff or hiring new staff.

4 Trial periods involve an applicant being employed for a short while to make sure they are capable of doing the job and are reliable. This avoids offering a job to someone who isn't suitable and having to go through dismissal proceedings.

5 Training schemes – intense programmes of training that equip staff with the skills to be in a good position for either a pay rise or a promotion.

   Work-based qualifications – offer staff the chance to gain qualifications while working, e.g. apprenticeship or professional accounting qualifications.

Essential question 4.1

Human Resources (HR) could use workforce planning to ensure that the organisation has the number of staff, with the correct skills, to meet the needs of the organisation at the time they are required.

HR could use methods of testing, such as aptitude tests, to ensure applicants for new positions have the required skills and abilities to work effectively in the organisation, e.g. giving an accountant a numerical test.

Answers

Key questions 4.2

1 Productivity and/or customer service will improve.

   There will be lower staff turnover (staff leaving and having to recruit new staff).

   Better employee relations (relationships between employees and management).

2 Commission – salespeople receive a percentage of the sales they make, which will motivate them to sell more.

   Performance related pay – an extra bonus payment on top of the basic wage is paid for meeting agreed targets.

3 According to McGregor, a Theory X employee is perceived to dislike work and avoid it at all costs *whereas* a Theory Y employee is perceived to be satisfied by their job and motivated to achieve personal and organisation goals.

4 Physiological needs – Staff need wages, a basic safe working environment, access to toilet facilities and running water, etc.

   Safety and security – Staff need a contract of employment to give them job security.

   Self-esteem – Staff are motivated by having an important job title and recognition of their achievements in front of peers.

5 According to Hertzberg, employees are motivated by two sets of factors. Hygiene factors will not motivate employees, but if ⇨

⇨ these are not met, they can *lower* motivation, for example, clean toilets. Motivator factors will not necessarily lower motivation if they are absent, but can be responsible for *increasing* motivation, e.g. promotion opportunities.

6 a) Autocratic – Authority and control is retained by the leader. Managers tell employees what to do.

   b) Democratic – Managers let employees have a say in decision-making.

   c) Laissez-faire – Managers do not issue instructions or supervise staff, they just let staff decide how to carry out tasks on their own.

Essential question 4.2

Setting up a works council/consultative committee, where an equal number of employees and managers have joint decision-making powers.

Paying employees a 'piece rate', which is paying per item produced and encourages a high work rate.

Answers

Key questions 4.3

1 An informal appraisal is a quick chat, while working or during a coffee break, highlighting something an employee is doing well or to give advice.

   A peer-to-peer appraisal is when the review is carried out by a colleague at the same level as the employee.

   A 360-degree appraisal involves the peer or line manager who conducts the appraisal, interviewing fellow employees, supervisors and subordinates about the performance of the employee.

2 a) ACAS is a government-funded organisation that attempts to solve disputes in the workplace to stop them going to court. ACAS stands for the Advisory, Conciliation and Arbitration service. It offers advice on all HR matters (advisory), listens to both sides of the dispute (conciliation), acts as an impartial referee (arbitration) and makes final decisions if agreed.

   b) CBI stands for the Confederation of British Industry. It is a powerful business group that represents many employers. The CBI can use its size and voice to campaign (known as 'lobbying') for government influence that will benefit its members.

   c) A trade union is an organisation that represents a group of employees. Employees benefit from standing together (collective bargaining), the experience of the union leaders and the legal powers the union has.

3 Employers must be able to give account of the policies the employee has broken and the procedures and sanctions that have been used before dismissal.

   Employers should use a fair and consistent procedure when dismissing employees.

4 A grievance is a concern, problem or complaint raised by an employee, for example, to do with working conditions, relationships with colleagues, or a complaint about their manager.

Essential question 4.3

Maintaining good employee relations by consulting with employees on any major changes that are about to take place, especially if it will impact on their working day, such as a new office layout or new procedures, will reduce the chances of employees resisting change. Negative employee relations can result in industrial action, such as a strike whereby employees refuse to work, which will result in no work being done, no goods being made or sold and customers going to the competition.

Answers

Key questions 4.4

1 Age, disability, gender.
2 Harassment – Behaviour that is deemed offensive by the recipient due to a protected characteristic.

 Victimisation – When someone is treated badly because they have made or supported a grievance under this legislation.

 Direct discrimination – Where someone is treated less favourably than another person because of a protected characteristic.
3 Permanent – Employment lasts until either party gives the required notice of termination.

Temporary – Employment is for a set period of time to fill a vacancy, such as maternity leave.

Fixed term – Employment for a fixed period, such as a seasonal contract for a summer job.

Essential questions 4.4

1 National Minimum Wage Act 1998.
2 The National Minimum Wage Act 1998 makes it illegal to pay an employee below a certain amount per hour as long as employees meet the age criteria to qualify for each minimum rate. Any increase to the minimum wage by the government will increase the costs to the business and so lower profits.

Answers

Key questions 5.1

1 External:
 ● Mortgage which is a loan secured on property.

 Internal:
 ● Using profits retained from previous years.
2 If the business needs short-term finance, it may get an overdraft, for example.

 If the business needs long-term finance, it may get a mortgage, for example.

 The interest rates need to be considered as the business will want to pay as little interest as possible.
3 A venture capitalist is a large organisation *whereas* a business angel is usually an individual. A venture capitalist invests very large amounts *whereas* a business angel invests smaller amounts. *Both* require an equity stake in the business.

4 Advantage: Guaranteed to get some money back.

 Disadvantage: Have to sell the debt to the factoring firm for less than it is worth.

Essential questions 5.1

1 A loan from a bank is paid back with interest added.

 Shares could be sold which are small fragments of ownership sold either privately or on the stock market.
2 A bank loan is paid back in manageable monthly instalments, which makes it easier to pay back and to budget for.

 Huge amounts of finance can be raised selling shares on the stock market, which can be used to grow the business, for example, to open new stores.

Answers

Key questions 5.2

1 Owners – to check profitability.

   HMRC – to check tax payments are correct.

   Employees – to check job security.

2 To compare their profitability with their rivals.

   To assess if rivals are ripe for a takeover.

3 An income statement shows revenue (sales), which is the amount of money received for selling goods and/or services during the year.

   It calculates the gross profit, which is the profit made from buying and selling stock.

   It also lists expenses, which are other costs incurred by the business.

4 Gross profit is the profit made from buying and selling stock *whereas* profit for the year is profit made after expenses are deducted from gross profit.

5 Working capital is current assets – current liabilities. This shows how easily a business can pay its short-term debts.

6 Cash budgets allow a manager to predict a surplus or a deficit. If a surplus is predicted it allows investment. If a deficit is predicted it allows action to be taken, such as arranging finance.

Essential question 5.2

An income statement calculates the profitability of the business by working out the Gross profit which is the profit made from buying and selling, and the overall Profit for the year (net profit) which is the profit once expenses are deducted from gross profit.

A statement of financial position calculates the value and worth of an organisation at a specific point in time. It shows what the organisation's assets and liabilities are.

Answers

Key questions 5.3

1 a) Liquidity ratios measure the ability of the business to pay its debts.

   b) Profitability ratios measure how profitable a business is by providing a percentage figure for comparison.

   c) Efficiency ratios measure how well a business uses its resources.

2 ROEE (Return on Equity Employed)

3 PFTY / capital × 100

Essential questions 5.3

1 a) Liquidity: current ratio.

   This measures an organisation's ability to pay off its short-term debts.

   The formula is: current assets / current liabilities.

   b) Profitability: gross profit ratio.

   This measures the percentage of profit made from buying and selling stock.

   The formula is: gross profit / sales revenue × 100.

   c) Efficiency: rate of inventory turnover.

   This shows how many times a business uses inventory in a year.

   The formula is: cost of sales / average inventory.

2 Uses: Easy to compare the financial performance of the business with previous years and compare financial performance with competitors.

   Limitations: Information in financial statements is historical so is not relevant to the current position or the future, which makes planning and decision-making difficult. Ratios also don't take external factors, for example, high interest rates resulting in low spending, into account.

Answers

Key questions 6.1

1 a) How do consumers purchase products, e.g. using a debit card?

   Where do consumers purchase products, e.g. using e-commerce?

   b) Possible answers could include: Need to promote products through point of sale merchandising and sales promotions.

   Need to provide payment services, e.g. contactless payment or e-commerce facilities.

2 Random sampling – choosing to survey anyone at random from an extensive list.

   Quota sampling – selecting respondents based on characteristics.

Cluster sampling – sampling from a small but representative area of the population.

3 Advantage: Using electronic point of sale means reactions to price changes can influence future pricing.

   Disadvantage: Money-off rewards can lower profits.

Essential question 6.1

Test marketing allows a product to be trialled in one area, which means the product can be adapted if necessary to allow a successful national launch.

Telephone surveys can be used to target specific area codes, which allows the business to meet the needs of local markets.

Answers

Key questions 6.2

1 a) Product endorsement involves the use of well-known celebrities to promote the product.

   b) Product placement involves products appearing in films, TV programmes or video games.

2 Sale or return involves products being sent back to the supplier at no cost if they cannot be sold.

   Credit terms allow businesses to pay for goods at a later date.

3 Catalogues allow customers to browse through products at home and order online or via telephone.

   Personal selling involves salespeople contacting customers directly to try and sell products.

4 The brand name of the product can be changed.

   New variations can be launched.

   The price could be lowered.

5 Press conferences involves the media being invited to a business presentation to be given information or news.

The business could sponsor a team or event.

The business could donate to charity.

6 a) Adding a percentage 'mark-up' to the unit cost of the product.

   b) Different prices for different types of customer, e.g. different ages.

7 Products can be distributed via the road networks direct to customers.

   Products can be distributed worldwide via airmail.

   Products and services can be distributed via utilities infrastructure, e.g. fibre-optic broadband.

8 Promotions should not mislead customers.

   Environmentally friendly claims should be accurate.

Essential questions 6.2

1 The price could be decreased. This would mean the product is more affordable to more market segments and so increase sales.

   The business could sell online using e-commerce. This would mean a worldwide market could be reached.

$\Rightarrow$

2 Advantages:

- A business can use newer products to replace those at the end of the product life cycle.
- *Cash cows* (high market share/low market growth) can be used to fund riskier ventures such as promoting stars (high market share/ high market growth) products to keep them ahead of the competition.

Disadvantages:

- Costs are high to research and develop a variety of products.
- *Dogs* (low market share/low market growth) can drain a business's profits unless they are sold off.

Answers

Key questions 6.3

1 Digital screens use moving images so are more likely to capture attention.

   Digital screens can play multiple adverts rather than just one poster.

2 Can be used to access the internet to purchase products through m-commerce.

   Can be used to purchase apps for businesses to target promotions and services to.

Can be used to access social media, which businesses can use to promote products on.

Essential question 6.3

The internet can be used to advertise products, targeted to customer wants through browsing histories.

Self-checkout systems can be used to speed up the process of purchasing products.

Answers

Key questions 7.1

1 Advantage – There are no wasted raw materials.

   Disadvantage – There could be the consequences of understocking, such as production stopping when raw materials run out unexpectedly or not being able to meet demand.

2 Logistics management ensures the right products are in the right place at the right time, at low cost.

   Logistics management also co-ordinates with the supply chain.

3 Labels should include maximum, minimum and re-order level. The X axis should be labelled 'Time' and the Y axis should be labelled 'Stock (or inventory) level'.

Essential questions 7.1

1 Maximum stock level – the most amount of stock a business should hold.

   Minimum stock level – the least amount of stock a business should hold.

2 So the business doesn't overstock, which means there is less chance of stock going out of date.

   So the business doesn't understock, which means they cannot satisfy demand, resulting in customers going elsewhere.

Answers

Key questions 7.2

1 So that enough goods are produced to meet anticipated sales.

   So enough supplies are ordered to avoid understocking.

2 Advantage – Humans can use initiative and creativity, which is often lacking in automated systems.

   Disadvantage – Humans have to take breaks, holidays, etc., which limits production time.

3 Employees become efficient at their role by repeating the same tasks routinely, often as a result of flow production.

Essential questions 7.2

1 Job production – This involves making unique one-off products to a customer's specifications.

Batch production – This is when groups of similar products are made at a time.

2 **Job production**

Advantage – Produces a unique, high-quality product which means high prices can be charged.

Disadvantage – The high skill of staff will mean high wages will need to be paid.

Batch production

Advantage – Can allow for changes to products to be made easily as all the machinery is standardised.

Disadvantage – Staff and machinery may be idle between batches, increasing costs.

Answers

Key questions 7.3

1 Poor quality goods can result in customer's returning their purchase, losing sales.

   High quality goods can result in a good reputation and new customers buying from the business.

2 Quality management:
   - involves everyone in the organisation focusing on quality
   - can involve a variety of quality methods such as quality assurance, quality circles and quality improvement (kaizen)
   - results in zero errors.

3 No bias is shown as the mystery shopper isn't employed by the business.

   Valuable feedback regarding whether or not a product or experience is satisfactory can be gathered.

Essential questions 7.3

1 Quality control involves inspecting finished goods and raw materials.

   Quality standards involves a product being awarded a symbol for meeting an agreed standard.

2 Quality control:
   - No unsatisfactory products are sold to customers, which means no products are returned.
   - The business does not end up with a bad reputation, as no faulty products are sold.

   Quality standards:
   - A symbol awarded for meeting standards can be used for marketing purposes, which can attract customers.
   - A higher price can be charged as the product is proven to be of high quality.

Answers

Key questions 7.4

1 Advantage – Fairtrade products can appeal to customers who appreciate the ethics of the product.

   Disadvantage – There can be less choice than with non-Fairtrade certified products.

2 Using EV (electric vehicles) for delivery vans or company cars results in zero-emissions.

   Using advances in renewable energy technology, such as wind or solar energy, to power factories or offices.

Essential question 7.4

CAM (computer aided manufacture) uses robotics to completely automate the production process.

Computerised inventory (stock) management systems can automatically re-order inventory.

Solutions to exam-style questions

Exam-style questions practice – Chapter 1

Example

Exam-style solutions

1. A PLC can sell shares to anyone through the stock market whereas an Ltd company can only sell shares to private individuals they know, such as employees.

   Both a PLC and a Ltd company have limited liability, which is when owners (shareholders) are only at risk of losing their investment and not personal possessions, if the business fails.

   Both a PLC and a Ltd company are controlled by a board of directors.

2. Social enterprises:
   - can attract customers who appreciate their social cause
   - can also attract good quality staff who want to work for an organisation that makes a difference
   - are likely to receive help from the government, for example, grants, because they impact positively on society
   - benefit from an asset lock, so the sale of assets, should they go bust, go to their good cause not to creditors.

3. Advantages:
   - Franchiser is able to grow with minimal risk.
   - Franchiser receives a share of the profits.

   Disadvantages:
   - If one individual franchise gets a bad reputation, it will affect the whole brand.
   - The franchiser misses out on all the profits they would make if they grew organically.

4. A multinational organisation:
   - has operations in more than one country
   - usually bases its head office in its home country
   - can influence governments and receive grants for creating jobs.

5. To grow organically, a business could:
   - launch new products/services which means businesses can meet the needs of different market segments
   - open new physical branches by opening up in new locations means they can reach new markets and more customers
   - introduce e-commerce, selling online which means the business can trade 24/7 around the world ⇨

Remember

... when the command word 'compare' is used, write *whereas* to make a point of distinction (differences) between two related factors and *both* to make a point of similarity between two related factors.

Remember

... when asked to 'explain' you must relate *cause* and *effect*. In answer 5, the *cause* is given first and the *effect* is then explained. Show the examiner you are explaining the *effect* by writing key linking phrases, such as 'this means,' 'meaning,' 'this will,' 'so,' etc. between the cause and the effect you explain.

$\Rightarrow$

- expand their existing premises which means they can have more products/staff and make more sales
- hire more staff; this will improve the business' ability to make more sales or develop more products.

6 Advantages:
- Outsourcing allows a business to concentrate on core activities.
- Less labour and equipment is required for outsourced activities, e.g. saving on printers and reprographics staff.
- An outsourced business may provide the service cheaper than in house as they can benefit from economies of scale.

Disadvantages:
- Communication between businesses needs to be very clear to make sure exact specifications are met.
- May have to share sensitive information.
- An outsourcing could be more expensive that in house as specialists and expertise come at a price.

7 Market share is an organisation's percentage of the overall sales in a particular market.

The organisation with the most market share is known as the market leader.

8 Each project team has staff from all functional areas which means a good amount of experience as skills in each team.

Complex problems can be solved as each team has decision makers with good skills and experience managing them.

Staff can use their expertise which means they feel valued and are motivated.

9 Decentralised management delegates decision-making to individual departments whereas centralised decision-making retains decision-making at head office.

Decentralised management results in the organisation losing an overall corporate image if each department/branch is operating differently, whereas with centralised management a high degree of corporate identity and strategy exists.

Decentralised management allows more subordinates to be empowered, whereas with centralised management less responsibility is given to subordinates.

10 Advantages:
- Each division can meet the needs of the local market which means customer loyalty will build up.
- The business can react to changing external (PESTEC) factors, such as competition cutting prices as each group is close to the local market.
- It is easy to identify a failing group which means divisional managers can be held accountable and changes can be made.

Disadvantages:
- Duplication of resources, such as administration staff or IT equipment across each group, which will increase costs to the organisation.

Exam-style questions practice – Chapter 2

Example

Exam-style solutions

1 If an organisation doesn't have available finance it may not be able to carry out decisions and courses of action it wishes to, such as expanding the business by developing new products.

The organisation won't be able to invest in new technology, such as e-commerce or robotics.

The organisation may have to take drastic action to cut costs, such as closing a branch, making staff redundancies or delayering.

2 Interest rates can increase which means customers have less disposable income to spend on a business' goods and services due to higher borrowing costs.

Interest rates can decrease which means customers are less likely to save because of unattractive rates and therefore will spend more on an organisation's products.

The economic cycle can affect an organisation in a positive way as during times of boom/recovery customers are more likely to spend because employment rates are higher, meaning sales will increase.

The economic cycle can affect an organisation in a negative way as during a recession unemployment is high which reduces disposable income. This means customers are less likely to spend, so sales will fall and, furthermore, the business may have to take drastic action, such as downsizing.

3 A positive corporate culture can make employees feel part of the organisation through the use of uniforms, jargon and language which will increase motivation.

A positive corporate culture will mean a lower staff turnover as employees will want to remain part of the organisation, therefore saving money on recruitment and training costs.

A business known for a positive corporate culture will attract the best staff because they want to be part of the organisation and to experience the culture.

A culture of openness and flexible working arrangements will mean staff work when and where suits them best and so will perform better.

Through rituals, such as 'dress down Friday', a relaxed environment can be created which means staff are more able to forge relationships which will encourage collaboration and increase both creativity and productivity.

4 Organisations cannot participate in colluding with other organisations to fix prices in cartels. ⇒

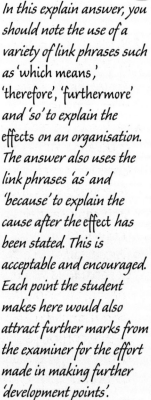

Hints & tips

In this explain answer, you should note the use of a variety of link phrases such as 'which means,' 'therefore', 'furthermore' and 'so' to explain the effects on an organisation. The answer also uses the link phrases 'as' and 'because' to explain the cause after the effect has been stated. This is acceptable and encouraged. Each point the student makes here would also attract further marks from the examiner for the effort made in making further 'development points'.

Organisations can have potential mergers blocked if the merge is likely to lower competition in the market substantially.

Organisations cannot use their dominant position in the market to charge drastically low prices, pay lower prices to suppliers or control the supply of goods.

5 Email can be used to communicate information regarding decisions to many employees at once.

4G will enable organisations' employees to communicate and download information while on the move much more quickly.

Video-conferencing can reduce the need for managers to travel to meetings, saving time and travel costs.

Robotics can improve the consistency and quality of production.

Exam-style questions practice – Chapter 3

Example

Exam-style solutions

1 A strategic decision is a long-term decision whereas an operational decision is a day-to-day decision.

A strategic decision is made by senior managers whereas an operation decision is made by all staff or low-level supervisors.

A strategic decision concerns the long-term objectives of the organisation, such as to grow, whereas an operational decision is to do with a routine task, such as staff lunch rotas.

2 Advantages of using a structured decision-making model, such as SWOT analysis are:
- It identifies strengths and allows a business to build upon them, for example, having a good brand name so launching new products within the brand.
- It identifies weaknesses and allows them to be addressed. For example, a poorly performing branch can be spotted and if downsizing is necessary, an under-performer can be closed.
- It identifies threats and allows them to be turned into opportunities, for example, by embracing advancing technology, not allowing it to leave the business behind.

However, disadvantages are:
- A SWOT analysis is very time consuming.
- A SWOT analysis is a very structured process which can stifle creativity and gut reactions from managers.

3 A manager has the following roles in an organisation:
- Plan: Looking ahead, seeing potential opportunities, or problems, setting targets and strategies.

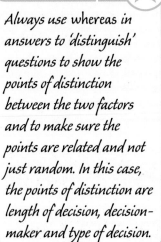

Hints & tips

Always use whereas in answers to 'distinguish' questions to show the points of distinction between the two factors and to make sure the points are related and not just random. In this case, the points of distinction are length of decision, decision-maker and type of decision.

- Command: Issuing instructions, informing staff, motivating staff.
- Co-ordinate: Bringing together the resources of the business to achieve the overall objectives.
- Control: Measuring and correcting the activities in the organisation. A manager looks at what is being done and checks it against what was expected.
- Delegate: Giving subordinates the authority to carry out management-level tasks. This helps lessen manager's workload and motivates staff.

4 Managers that have the ability and experience to make good decisions, are willing to take risk, and are empowered to make decisions.

Staff resistance to change can stop a decision being actioned.

Financial constraints may mean that the organisation cannot choose the best solution to a problem.

The quality of the information available on which to base the decision may be poor, e.g. out of date, biased, not relevant, etc.

5 Spreadsheets can improve the accuracy of calculations because formula can perform 'What if?' statements to calculate the projected outcome of a decision.

Databases can improve the speed of decision-making as it is possible to search for information quickly using queries and sort functions.

Email can be used to send attachments containing information which means printing costs are reduced.

Video-conferencing can reduce the need for managers to travel to meetings where decisions will be made, which saves time and travel costs.

Hints & tips

Try to avoid repeating the same points. If you do, make sure they are explained in a way that makes them obviously different, as in the two cost-saving advantages in solution 5.

Exam-style questions practice – Chapter 4

Example

Exam-style solutions

1 Employees could 'go slow'. This is working at a slower rate than normal which means the rate of production will slow down.

Employees could refuse to do any overtime so the organisation won't be able to fulfil any rush orders or cope with increased demand.

Employees could work to rule. This involves employees only completing the statutory duties outlined in their contracts. This means the organisation will be less responsive to change, for example, employees won't volunteer for extra training courses to use the latest technology.

Finally, an organisation could see a positive impact on morale because the industrial action is successful and employers agree to a pay rise, for example.

2 **a)**
- The task itself will affect the leadership style. A complex task will require more direction from management, so an autocratic style would be required. A creative task would benefit from a hands-off approach, so a laissez-faire style would be better suited.
- There may be less time to complete a project so a more direct, autocratic style will be required.
- Highly skilled and competent staff will need less supervision, leading to democratic or laissez-faire styles being chosen.
- Poorly motivated employees cannot be trusted to have the self-discipline to make their own decisions and complete tasks without instruction and supervision, so autocratic leadership will be chosen.

b)
- With an autocratic style, control over tasks and instructions is retained by the leader, whereas with laissez-faire, control is delegated to employees who set their own tasks.
- An autocratic style can demotivate staff as there are fewer opportunities for delegation and empowerment, whereas with a laissez-faire style staff are highly empowered and likely to be more motivated at work.

3 Worker-directors are a low-level employee being given a seat on the board of directors. This means employees feel that they have a voice in decision-making.

Works councils/consultative committees are groups made up of an equal number of employees and managers to discuss major suggestions for change in the organisation. Therefore resistance to change from employees is reduced as employees have had a say in deciding the changes that are made.

4 Flexitime – Employees choose their own hours through flexitime. An advantage of this is that employees can't be disciplined for poor timekeeping as long as they work their contracted hours. However, a disadvantage is that it is difficult to arrange formal meetings <u>unless 'core time' is set, which means that employees must be in the office during certain times</u>.

Working from home – Employees can work from home but keep in touch via the use of ICT, such as email. An advantage of this is employees can save on travel time which means that they can get more work done instead of having 'dead-time' traveling to the office. However, one disadvantage is it is difficult to supervise the quality of homeworkers. Another disadvantage is relationships with colleagues and managers can break down if employees are often away from the office.

Hints & tips ⭐

If you can, give development points in all questions. The third sentence in the first bullet point here would receive an extra mark.

Hints & tips ⭐

Remember to focus your 'discuss' answers on arguments for and against, that is advantages and disadvantages. Extra marks can be gained, however, for developing your points, including giving examples and drawing conclusions. The underlined section here would get an extra mark.

5 If employee relations are negative, employees will leave for a better work environment. This increases staff turnover which will, in turn, mean an increase in training and recruitment/selection costs.

Negative employee relations result in less co-operation from staff which will make changes harder to introduce and once introduced will be more likely to be unsuccessful.

There will be an increase in grievances which ties up managers' time to deal with them.

In extreme cases industrial action will take place which could give the business a bad reputation, meaning they will find it hard to recruit quality staff in the future.

6 The advantages of external recruitment are:
- Fresh, new ideas and skills are brought into the organisation.
- Recruiting from outside the organisation avoids creating a further vacancy in the organisation as promotion would.
- Jealousy and resistance are avoided as one employee is not being promoted over others.

The disadvantages of external recruitment are:
- Candidates don't know the organisation so induction training will have to be carried out.
- The organisation does not know the candidate, which carries a risk that they may not be suited for the job or are untrustworthy.
- Existing staff may be de-motivated as there are no internal promotion prospects.

7 An employee must be given a written contract of employment particulars within two months of starting. This contract will state rate of pay, hours and holiday entitlement.

Employees have a right to an itemised pay slip stating their wages, tax deductions, etc.

Employees have the right to maternity and paternity leave.

Employees have the right to request flexible working.

> **Hints & tips** ⭐
>
> There is nothing wrong with a bulleted list like this, as long as each bullet is written in a proper sentence.

Exam-style questions practice – Chapter 5

Example

Exam-style solutions

1 Businesses could offer cash discounts to customers. This means customers are more likely to pay with cash rather than credit, which will give the business more cash.

Businesses should seek credit from suppliers which means they avoid spending their cash reserves and can pay once they have sales revenue.

> **Remember** 📌
>
> ... with 'explain' questions, give the effect and explain the cause or give the cause and explain the effect.

Use just-in-time (JIT) stock control. This involves only ordering stock when it is needed for production, which will improve cash flow because it will not tie up money in stock that is not being used.

Offer promotions such as buy one get one free (BOGOF), which will increase the revenue brought in through sales.

The business could arrange finance, such as an overdraft or bank loan. This means they will have the funds available to pay suppliers and avoid running up debts.

2 Income statement (trading, profit and loss account) shows:
- Gross profit which is the money made from buying and selling stock.
- Profit for the year (net profit) which is the profit made after expenses are deducted.

Statement of financial position (balance sheet) shows:
- The assets the business owns and the liabilities it owes.
- The total value of the business, known as total net assets.

3 a)
- Debentures are loans from individuals to gain finance, whereas shares involve giving ownership to individuals in return for investment to gain finance.
- Debenture holders receive interest payments, whereas shareholders receive dividend payments.

   b)
- Current ratio measures the ability to pay off short-term debts, whereas the acid test ratio measures the ability to pay off short-term debts in a crisis situation.
- The ideal current ratio result is 2:1, whereas the acid test ratio result is acceptable at 1:1.

4 Plan – Carry out cash budgets to aid future decision-making.
Organise – Arrange for the finance to be in place to give the business funds.
Command – Inform staff of the need to cut costs to improve the financial position.
Co-ordinate – Ensuring staff, for example, accountants, have support and are on task.
Control – Studying financial statements to control costs, such as expenses.
Delegate – Give departments responsibility for their own budgets.
Motivate – Analyse the cash budgets to assess if pay rises can be offered to employees.

5 a)
- Ratios don't take internal factors (e.g. staff motivation or staff turnover) into account.
- Must compare like for like when comparing with competitors and it is unlikely both firms will be of the same size and type.

Remember

… POCCCDM is a great way to answer this question about the role of a manager, but remember it has to be in context of the question, that is relevant to the department you are asked about; in this case the finance department. If you cannot do that, general roles such as monitor cash flow, monitor performance and forecast trends, etc. are accepted answers too.

⇨
- Ratios don't take new product development or recent product launches into account.

b) Gross profit ratio: ESQ Ltd = 17%, competition = 29%
- ESQ Ltd has a much lower GP percentage than the competition. ESQ Ltd could find a cheaper supplier which would lower the cost of sales and therefore improve gross profit.
- It could also look for the marketing department to cut prices, offer discounts or special offers which will increase revenue generated through sales.

Current ratio: ESQ Ltd = 6.8 : 1, competition = 2.3 : 1

- ESQ Ltd actually has too high a Current Ratio because the ideal ratio is around 2:1, which the competition has, so they should look to lower the figure.
- ESQ Ltd may have too many current assets, such as cash which they could invest, for example, in developing new products, meaning the cash could be used to grow the business.

Hints & tips ⭐

In question 5a, one common answer given by students (that is, information being historical) has been excluded in the question wording to make it a bit more difficult to answer. This is quite common in Higher Business Management, so be sure to read the question thoroughly.

Exam-style questions practice – Chapter 6

Example

Exam-style solutions

1 Advantages:
   - Desk research is cost effective because information is free to gather using published materials.
   - Desk research is quick to gather which allows the business to spend time on other activities such as developing products.

   Disadvantages:
   - However, desk research might be biased as it was collated by someone else.
   - Desk research may also not be appropriate to the business' needs because it was gathered for another purpose.

2 The demand for a product will affect the pricing strategy. If demand is high, the business can set prices high. On the other hand, if demand is low, the price should be set lower to encourage sales.

   If the product is targeted at a wealthy market segment, the price should be higher.

   The unit cost of the product should be considered and the price set higher than that.

   External factors will affect prices, for example, a boom period in the economy should see prices rise.

3 There has been a trend in out-of-town retail parks that have large stores, free car parking and are close to road networks. ⇨

Remember

...you can add a development point for an extra mark as seen in the first point of answer 2.

There has also been a trend in convenience supermarkets, situated in busy places such as city centres and train stations which people can get to easily.

There has been a trend in massive hypermarkets that sell many goods and services under one roof.

4 A retailer has the advantage of not having to pay for storing many items at once.

A retailer can take advantage of promotions offered by wholesalers that manufacturers may not offer.

However, a retailer will have to pay more for products as the wholesaler will add a margin of profit on top.

The retailer may also miss out on exclusivity deals offered by manufacturers.

5 a) Development: The business actually makes a loss at this stage as the product isn't on sale and the costs of research and development (R&D) are high. Sales are zero because the product hasn't been launched onto the market yet.

b) Growth: Profits are low because promotion costs are high to raise awareness of the product. Sales are being made but progress is slow as customers are still unsure of the new product.

c) Saturation: Profits begin to fall as the market has attracted many competitor products. Sales also begin to fall, although extension strategies could be used, such as lowering the price, which will encourage extra sales.

6 a)
- Market-led businesses develop products based on customer wants whereas product-led businesses produce products that they believe customers will want and try to convince them to buy them.
- Market-led businesses rely heavily on market research whereas product-led businesses focus more on product research and development.

b)
- Above-the-line (ATL) promotions use mass media to advertise products whereas below-the-line (BTL) promotions do not use mass media.
- Both ATL and BTL promotions aim to raise awareness of products and encourage sales.

7 Through social media:
- Users 'like' or 'follow' the business' page so businesses can target customers or potential customers easily.
- Businesses can let customers know of new products or promotions using social media.
- Customers can leave comments, allowing simple and effective market research.

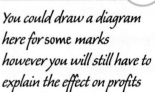

Hints & tips

Note the subtle use of the word however *to indicate that the discussion is changing to disadvantages.*

Hints & tips

You could draw a diagram here for some marks however you will still have to explain the effect on profits and sales at each stage.

- However, a disadvantage is customers can leave negative comments for all to see too.

Using apps:

- A business can target promotions to customers based on their browsing history.
- Services can be offered for a fee, such as music downloads or products sold via m-commerce.

8 Customers anywhere in the world can purchase products, meaning a world-wide customer reach.

Online discounts can be offered which will attract customers away from more expensive retail outlets.

Customers can access product information immediately, for example, stock availability, which means customers save time on fruitless trips to retail outlets.

There's more choice for customers online than a high street outlet could stock and display because an entire range of products can be shown.

Exam-style questions practice – Chapter 7

 Example

Exam-style solutions

1 Staff – If the workforce is highly skilled, their expertise would be better suited to job production. Also, rising labour costs, perhaps due to a rising minimum wage, could mean that the business should move to capital-intensive production.

   Finance – Large amounts of finance are required to equip factories or hire enough staff needed for large-scale flow production.

   Technology – If the business does not have the technology required for capital-intensive production, then labour-intensive production is the only option.

2 a) Capital intensive involves using mostly machinery to produce goods, whereas labour intensive is using mostly human labour to produce goods. Capital intensive can use CAM and robotics which can work 24/7, whereas the humans used in labour intensive need breaks and holidays, so achieving 24/7 production is not as easy.

   b) Both mechanisation and automation involve using machinery to produce goods. Mechanisation still involves labour to control the machinery, whereas automation produces goods independently of human control.

3 The relationships with suppliers will need to be considered as if they are not good a high minimum stock level will need to be set to ensure there is a supply of materials should deliveries be late.

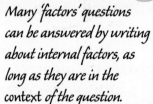

Hints & tips

Many 'factors' questions can be answered by writing about internal factors, as long as they are in the context of the question.

The skill levels of staff will need to be high because materials cannot be wasted if a very low level is set.

The finance available will need to be considered as if cash flow is an issue a low minimum level will tie less money up in stock.

4 Advantages:
- Employees are motivated by being involved in decision-making.
- The business gets feedback from those actually producing the products.
- Employee relations are improved by staff and management working together.

Disadvantages:
- Employees meet during company time, impacting on production.
- Employees have to be trained to join a quality circle, taking even more time away from production.

5 Multinationals can use large centralised warehouses all over the world as they are built near good infrastructure links such as motorways, airports and docks.

Large centralised warehouses can allow the business to benefit from economies of scale through bulk buying.

Centralised warehouses allow for the same consistent procedures to be used all over the world.

Unlike many smaller warehouses in many different countries security against theft is tightened.

6 Products should consider animal welfare issues such as not testing on animals. This means they may be awarded the 'leaping bunny' logo, which can be used for marketing purposes.

The operations department could use fair-trade suppliers or stock fair-trade products, which means they will attract customers who appreciate their ethical stance.

Renewable energies, for example, wind energy, can be used to power factories and offices which will save costs in the long run.

Waste should be disposed of appropriately which will avoid any prosecutions and time-consuming inspections from environmental regulators.

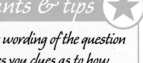

Hints & tips

The wording of the question gives you clues as to how many advantages and disadvantages you need. In this case both are plural so you need to include at least two of each in your answer.